I0439678

S. HRG. 113–475

TRANSATLANTIC SECURITY CHALLENGES: CENTRAL AND EASTERN EUROPE

HEARING

BEFORE THE

SUBCOMMITTEE ON EUROPEAN AFFAIRS

OF THE

COMMITTEE ON FOREIGN RELATIONS
UNITED STATES SENATE

ONE HUNDRED THIRTEENTH CONGRESS

SECOND SESSION

APRIL 10, 2014

Printed for the use of the Committee on Foreign Relations

Available via the World Wide Web: http://www.gpo.gov/fdsys/

U.S. GOVERNMENT PRINTING OFFICE

91–297 PDF   WASHINGTON : 2014

CONTENTS

(III)

TRANSATLANTIC SECURITY CHALLENGES: CENTRAL AND EASTERN EUROPE

THURSDAY, APRIL 10, 2014

U.S. SENATE,
SUBCOMMITTEE ON EUROPEAN AFFAIRS,
COMMITTEE ON FOREIGN RELATIONS,
Washington, DC.

The committee met, pursuant to notice, at 3:16 p.m., in room SD–419, Dirksen Senate Office Building, Hon. Christopher Murphy (chairman of the subcommittee) presiding.

Present: Senators Murphy, Cardin, and Johnson.

OPENING STATEMENT OF HON. CHRISTOPHER MURPHY, U.S. SENATOR FROM CONNECTICUT

Senator MURPHY. This hearing of the Senate Foreign Relations Subcommittee on European Affairs will now come to order. I would like to welcome everyone here today and explain our situation just very briefly. We are in a quorum call to try to figure out a path forward with respect to votes on the floor of the Senate. Senator Johnson and I have managed to escape that quorum call, but others of our colleagues are likely caught on the floor. We may be joined by a few others, but we decided to move forward with the hearing notwithstanding some of the activity on the floor.

This is a hearing today on transatlantic security challenges in Central and Eastern Europe. I would like to welcome our witnesses today on our first panel. We have two people that are no strangers to this committee, Assistant Secretary of State Victoria Nuland and Assistant Secretary of Defense Derek Chollet. On the second panel we are going to hear from Julianne Smith, Ian Brzezinski, and Edward Chow, all of whom I will introduce later.

Russia's invasion and illegal annexation of Crimea has called into question one of the key assumptions and underpinnings of 21st century transatlantic security strategy that Russia no longer poses a security threat to the alliance, and that the main challenges facing the allies emanate from beyond the Euro-Atlantic region. The winding down of the Afghanistan mission has led many to wonder if NATO, which has been the cornerstone of transatlantic reliance, would cease to be relevant. Instead, Russia's belligerent behavior may serve to reinvigorate the alliance. As Ambassador Ivo Daalder observed recently, "NATO has stood the test of time. Mr. Putin has just ensured that it will continue to do so."

The most immediate security challenge in Europe is the presence of tens of thousands of troops amassed on Russia's border with Ukraine. It is unclear whether President Putin plans to invade

Eastern Ukraine and seize control of the country or simply use the troop presence and advance teams of provocateurs to destabilize Ukraine until a friendly government can be installed in Kiev.

But recent events have crystallized many of the familiar debates about transatlantic security challenges. In addition, calls for increased defense spending, improved coordination, and the need to prioritize territorial defense and energy security are increasingly at the center of this conversation when we talk about security and the vulnerabilities of Central and Eastern Europe.

We call this hearing today to get an update on the administration's response to the crisis in Ukraine and to discuss how the United States and our allies can deter further Russian aggression, reassure our allies, and continue to help countries in the region become strong, prosperous independent democracies. The goal of our strategy must remain as always to make Europe, whole, free, and at peace.

Let me just very quickly suggest a few unequivocal steps that we can take to increase security and maybe have our panelists comment on them. First, as part of an increased NATO response, I think the United States should consider increasing troop levels in the region. Secretary Hagel has already said that a third brigade is being considered, and it is time for the United States to reevaluate our historically low U.S. force strength in Europe. Even a small increase will send a clear message to our friends and our adversaries. As this committee's great Dr. Brzezinski once said, "A trip wire has the same effect as a fence. It makes for more stable, neighborly relations."

Second, the United States and our European allies should suspend arms sales to Russia. I have joined several of my Senate colleagues in calling for the U.S. Government to end our business relationship with Russia's state Arms Export Agency, and I also hope that France will strongly reconsider the delivery of missile-class warships that were designed specifically for the type of invasion that just occurred on the shores of Crimea.

Third, now is the time for NATO to approve a membership action plan for Georgia. If the fear of confrontation over Georgia has divided our allies in the past, imagine the message that it will send to Mr. Putin that not only will he fail to achieve his objectives through threats and bullying, but that it is actually counterproductive. I hope that the administration will make a map for Georgia a priority at the upcoming NATO summit in Wales.

I will now turn to Senator Johnson for opening comments.

OPENING STATEMENT OF HON. RON JOHNSON, U.S. SENATOR FROM WISCONSIN

Senator JOHNSON. Thank you, Mr. Chairman. And, of course, when we were over in Ukraine we saw the very sobering situation therein. And this hearing we are facing the reality, and I think that is the primary thing we have to do here in the United States is we have to face some pretty harsh realities. And tough talk is fine, but Vladimir Putin really responds to only one thing, action. And I am glad, Mr. Chairman, that you are laying out some concrete actions we can take to change Vladimir Putin's calculus.

We need to deter Vladimir Putin, and we need to do that in a very forthright and resolved way, and the sooner the better because, Ms. Nuland, as you spoke earlier is that, you know, obviously making sure that Ukraine is successful is the best long-term strategy. We have a short-term problem, and we need to change Vladimir Putin's calculus now so that he does not go any further.

So with that, just looking forward to the testimony and appreciate you coming here to provide that testimony. Thank you.

Senator MURPHY. Both our witnesses are well known to the committee, so I will not trouble you to read you your own bios. We will start with Secretary Nuland and then move onto Secretary Chollet. Welcome again.

STATEMENT OF HON. VICTORIA NULAND, ASSISTANT SECRETARY OF STATE FOR EUROPEAN AND EURASIAN AFFAIRS, U.S. DEPARTMENT OF STATE, WASHINGTON, DC

Ms. NULAND. Thank you, Chairman Murphy, Ranking Member Johnson. I am honored to be here today to testify on the security challenges facing the transatlantic community in Central and Eastern Europe. Before I do that, I just want to take this opportunity to congratulate my friend and colleague, Assistant Secretary Chollet, on the arrival of his newest member of his family, Erin Chollet Hasta.

For over 20 years the United States and our European allies have worked to integrate Russia more closely into the Euro-Atlantic community through our bilateral engagement and organizations like the OSCE, the WTO, and the NATO-Russia Council. But Russia's actions in Ukraine over the last months are an affront to this effort and fundamentally change the security landscape of Eastern and Central Europe. Today I appreciate the opportunity to discuss the impact of Russia's actions on Ukraine, our policy response to that action, and other challenges in the region.

Russia's occupation of Crimea, rubber stamped by an illegitimate referendum conducted at the barrel of a gun, has tarnished its credibility and diminished its international standing in the eyes of Ukrainians and the world. This week's violent occupation of government buildings in Kharkhiv, Donetsk, and Luhansk deepen our concern.

Today, Ukraine is a frontline state in the struggle for freedom and all the principles that the transatlantic community holds dear. The United States stands with Ukraine in its effort to forge its own path forward to a more peaceful, free, and unified future. And we are very grateful to the members of this committee, including our chairman and our ranking member, for their attention to Ukraine and their travel and support for the people of Ukraine.

Our policy approach includes four basic pillars. First, our bilateral and multilateral support for Ukraine. Second, the costs we are imposing on Russia for its aggressive actions. Third, our efforts to de-escalate the crisis diplomatically. And fourth, our unwavering commitment to the security of our NATO allies who also live on the front lines of this crisis. Let me address the first three briefly, and Assistant Secretary Chollet will address the fourth in his testimony.

First, we support the Ukrainian people and the transitional government in the courageous steps they are taking to restore economic health, democratic choice, and internal stability and security to the country. The Rada has passed landmark anticorruption measures, deficit-reduction measures, and taken very difficult steps to reform the energy sector. Many of these will be painful for the Ukrainian people, but they are absolutely necessary, and they open the way to an IMF package of up to $18 billion in support.

The United States own $1 billion loan guarantee will help these reforms and will cushion some of the impact on the most vulnerable members of Ukrainian society. And we thank the Congress for its support of that loan guarantee. We are also using more than $100 million in bilateral support to assist Ukraine in strengthening anticorruption efforts, improving transparency, and helping the Ukrainian people prepare for free, fair elections on May 25.

Second, Russia is paying a very high price already for its actions, and that cost will go up if its pressure on Ukraine does not abate. Sanctions that we have already put in place are biting on the Russia economy, and we are now considering further measures in response to Russia's continued pressure on Ukraine. At the same time, we want to try to de-escalate the crisis diplomatically, if it at all possible. After many weeks of refusing to speak directly to Ukraine, the Russians have now agreed to sit down next week in a quadrilateral format, including Ukraine, the EU, and the United States, to discuss de-escalation, de-mobilization, support for elections, and constitutional reform. We will see how that session goes.

We are also concerned about the pressure this crisis is putting on Moldova, on Georgia, on Armenia, on Azerbaijan, and on other neighbors of Ukraine. Moldova in particular has been the victim of economic pressure from Russia, intense Russian-sponsored propaganda against its choice to associate with the EU, and renewed separatist efforts in Transnistria and Gagauzia. So we are very grateful that you, Mr. Ranking Member, are going to travel next week to, or this weekend, I think, to Moldova. They will very much appreciate the support. As you know, we have intensified United States political and economic support to Moldova and to the other states of the region in recent months, and this effort will be sustained.

The Ukraine crisis highlights another deep and growing challenge in the Euro-Atlantic space. The Maidon protestors had many grievances, but one of the most galvanizing across Ukraine was the pervasive corruption that has infused every aspect of Ukraine society, its economy, and its politics. As Secretary Kerry highlighted at the Munich Security Conference, we are seeing a similar disturbing trend in too many parts of Central and Eastern Europe and the Balkans now where the aspirations of citizens are being trampled beneath corrupt oligarchic interests who use their money and their influence to stifle political opposition and dissent, to buy politicians and media outlets, and to weaken judicial independence and the rights of NGOs.

We are also seeing a growing league of these oligarchs and corrupt politicians who are working together, including across national lines, to protect and help each other maintain that influence, and to keep the cash flowing that fees their preferred oligarchical system. Corruption of this kind does not simply rot democracies from the inside, it also makes them vulnerable to corrupting influences from the outside of the country who may seek undue economic or political influence over state policies and decisionmaking. In other words, in many parts of Europe, fighting corruption needs to be a higher national priority in order to protect and defend democracy and protect and defend state sovereignty.

As we look to shore up security, prosperity, and the values that are so vital to our shared aspiration for a Europe whole, free, and at peace, therefore, fighting corruption must be a more central line of effort, and it will be for our Bureau going forward. Similarly, the Ukraine crisis is a wake-up call to accelerate other work we have been doing to promote a stronger, more prosperous transatlantic community.

As Assistant Secretary Chollet will discuss, the renewed need for security vigilance along NATO's eastern border means that our European allies must reverse the downward trend in their defense budgets. And as we revitalize the transatlantic security tie, we must also strengthen our economic ties, and accelerate the growth and job creation on both sides of the Atlantic by completing an ambitious trade and investment partnership agreement.

Finally, as you said, Mr. Chairman, we must do more together as a transatlantic community to strengthen Europe's energy independence and its internal energy market, including by guaranteeing reverse flows of energy, ensuring greater diversity of supply, and building interconnectors throughout the continent. So this crisis has intensified our focus not just on Central and Eastern Europe, but on a broad set of transatlantic security challenges and opportunities on the road to a Europe whole, free, and at peace.

We are very grateful for the bipartisan and very active support of this subcommittee and the whole committee in that effort. I look forward to your questions.

[The prepared statement of Ms. Nuland follows:]

PREPARED STATEMENT OF ASSISTANT SECRETARY VICTORIA NULAND

Chairman Murphy and Ranking Member Johnson—I am honored to be here today to testify on the security challenges facing the transatlantic community in Central and Eastern Europe. Let me begin by thanking you for your leadership in the passage of the Support for the Sovereignty, Integrity, Democracy and Economic Stability of Ukraine Act. This legislation, which was supported by every member of this subcommittee, will enable the United States to provide needed help to Ukraine as the country undertakes its difficult transition.

I would also like to thank you for your visits to the region. I know that Chairman Murphy and Senator McCain have traveled to Kiev twice in the past 5 months, and that Senator McCain—along with Ranking Member Johnson, Senator Barrasso, and others—will travel to the Baltic States and Moldova this weekend. This engagement demonstrates America's continuing bipartisan support for a Europe whole, free, and at peace.

For over 20 years, the United States and our European allies have worked to integrate Russia more closely into the Euro-Atlantic community through our bilateral engagement and organizations like the OSCE, the WTO and the NATO-Russia Council. Russia's actions in Ukraine are an affront to this effort and fundamentally change the security landscape of Eastern and Central Europe. Today I appreciate the opportunity to discuss the impact of Russia's actions on Ukraine, our policy response to their actions and other challenges in the region.

Russia's occupation of Crimea, rubberstamped by an illegitimate referendum conducted at the barrel of a gun, has tarnished its credibility and diminished its international standing in the eyes of Ukrainians and the world. Reports of human rights abuses in Crimea since the Russian occupation have shocked the conscience. Russia has also attempted to intimidate Ukrainians by amassing more than 40 thousand troops and quick strike aircraft along the border, and with trade blockades and gas price hikes of 80 percent.

This week's violent occupation of government buildings in Kharkhiv, Donetsk, and Luhansk deepen our concern. Far from a spontaneous set of events, these incidents bear all the hallmarks of an orchestrated campaign of incitement, separatism and sabotage of the Ukrainian state, aided and abetted by the Russian security services.

So today Ukraine is a frontline state in the struggle for freedom and all the principles the transatantic community holds dear. The United States stands with Ukraine in its efforts to forge its own path forward to a more free, peaceful, and unified future. Our approach includes four pillars: first, our bilateral and multilateral support for Ukraine; second, the costs we are imposing on Russia for its aggressive actions; third, our efforts to deescalate the crisis diplomatically; and fourth, our unwavering commitment to the security of our NATO allies who also live on the front lines of this crisis. Let me address the first three briefly. Assistant Secretary Chollet will address the fourth in his testimony.

First, we support the Ukrainian people and the transitional government in the courageous steps they are taking to restore economic health, democratic choice, and internal stability and security to the country. The Rada has passed landmark anticorruption measures, deficit reduction measures and taken difficult steps to reform the energy sector. These necessary reforms will require painful sacrifices from all Ukrainians. But they also open the way to an IMF package of up to $18 billion in support.

The United States stands ready to help as the country addresses its immense challenges. Our $1 billion loan guarantee, in conjunction with IMF and EU assistance, will help implement these reforms and will cushion some of impact on the most vulnerable in Ukrainian society.

And we have approximately $92 million in FY 2013 State/USAID funding and an anticipated $86 million in FY 2014 State/USAID funding for assistance to Ukraine in areas such as strengthening anticorruption efforts, revising public procurement legislation, introducing agriculture and energy sector reforms, deepening privatization efforts, improving the transparency and quality of higher education and helping Ukraine prepare for free, fair elections on May 25.

We are also working with the international community to push back against Russian propaganda, lies and efforts to destabilize Ukraine's regions. The OSCE has already deployed more than 120 monitors in 10 locations throughout Ukraine as part of a special monitoring mission and the mandate allows the mission to grow to 500. The OSCE Office for Democratic Institutions and Human Rights will also play an essential role by sending 1,000 observers for the Presidential election, one of its biggest missions ever.

Second, Russia is already paying a high price for its actions, and that cost will go up if its pressure on Ukraine does not abate. Across the board, Russia has found itself isolated. The United States along with all other G7 members declined to attend the Sochi G8 summit and suspended participation in G8 activities. Instead, the G7 will meet in Brussels. On March 27, the United States and 99 other countries in the U.N. General Assembly reaffirmed the unity and territorial integrity of Ukraine within its internationally recognized borders. Only 11 voted against. Along with our allies, we have suspended practical cooperation between NATO and Russia. We have suspended most bilateral economic and military cooperation and much of the work of the U.S.-Russia Bilateral Presidential Commission. The President signed two Executive orders authorizing sanctions against those responsible, and finding that the actions and policies of the Russian government undermine democratic process and institutions in Ukraine; threaten its peace, security, stability, sovereignty, and territorial integrity; and contribute to the misappropriation of its assets. These sanctions have been carefully coordinated with the EU and other global partners. And today we are considering further measures in response to Russia's continued pressure on Ukraine.

And the financial markets are reacting. The ruble has fallen. Capital flight from Russia is at a high not seen in years. And Russia has been downgraded by major credit rating agencies on account of its actions.

These costs will only increase if Russia does not change course.

At the same time, we want to try to de-escalate the crisis. Secretary Kerry has met three times with Russian Foreign Minister Lavrov in recent weeks, with the support of the Ukrainian Government at a time when Russia would not meet directly with Ukraine. Earlier this week, Russia agreed to sit down next week with Ukraine, the EU, and United States to discuss de-escalation, demobilization, support for elections and constitutional reform. Between now and then, we have made it clear that Russia needs to take concrete steps to disavow separatist actions in

Eastern Ukraine, pull back its forces outside the country, and demonstrate that they are prepared to come to these discussions with the goal of de-escalating the conflict.

So Russia has a choice—to work with the international community to help build an independent Ukraine that can meet the hopes and aspirations of all Ukrainians, or Russia can face greater isolation and economic cost.

We are also concerned about the pressure this crisis is putting on Moldova, Georgia, Armenia, Azerbaijan, and other neighbors of Ukraine. Moldova in particular has been the victim of economic pressure from Russia, intense Russia-sponsored propaganda against its choice to associate with the EU and renewed separatist efforts in Transnistria and Gagauzia. As you know, we have intensified United States political and economic support to Moldova, and other states of the region in recent months and this effort will be sustained.

The Ukraine crisis highlights another deep and growing challenge in the Euro-Atlantic space. The Maidan protestors had many grievances. But one of the most galvanizing across Ukraine was the pervasive corruption that has infused every aspect of Ukraine's politics, economy, and social fabric for too long. And as Secretary Kerry highlighted at the Munich Security Conference, we are seeing a similar disturbing trend in too many parts of Central and Eastern Europe and the Balkans now ''where the aspirations of citizens are . . . being trampled beneath corrupt, oligarchic interests'' who ''use their money and influence to stifle political opposition and dissent, to buy politicians and media outlets, weaken judicial independence and the rights on NGOs.''

We are also seeing a growing league of oligarchs and corrupt politicians work together, including across national lines, to protect and help each other maintain that influence, and keep the cash flowing that feeds their preferred system. Corruption of this kind doesn't just rot democracies from the inside, it also makes them vulnerable to corrupting influences outside country who seek undue economic and political influence over state policies and decisionmaking. In other words, in many parts of Europe, fighting corruption needs to be a higher national priority in order to protect and defend democracy and state sovereignty.

As we look to shore up the security, prosperity, and values that are vital to our shared aspiration for a Europe whole, free, and at peace, therefore, fighting corruption must be a more central line of effort. Over the coming year, you will see our focus on this intensify in the work we do across the Balkans, and Central and Eastern Europe, in close collaboration with the with EU, to help these countries promote clean, accountable government, a lively and free civil society, and media independence and to help governments and citizens expose and root out corruption wherever it hides.

Similarly, the Ukraine crisis is a wake-up call to accelerate other work we have been doing to promote a stronger, more prosperous transatlantic community. As Assistant Secretary Chollet will discuss, the renewed need for security vigilance along NATO's Eastern border means our European allies must reverse the downward trend of shrinking defense budgets.

And even as we revitalize our transatlantic security ties, we must also strengthen our economic ties and accelerate the growth and job creation on both sides of the Atlantic by completing an ambitious Trans-Atlantic Trade and Investment Partnership agreement. The work that Eurozone countries are doing to strengthen the banking system and institute other reforms will also give investors confidence.

Finally, we must do more together as a transatlantic community to strengthen Europe's energy independence and internal market including guaranteeing reverse flow capabilities; ensuring greater diversity of supply; enhancing storage capacity and developing a deeper network of import terminals and interconnectors throughout the continent.

So this crisis has intensified our focus not just on Central and Eastern Europe but on a broad set of transatlantic security challenges—and opportunities—on the road to a Europe whole, free, and at peace.

We are grateful for the bipartisan and very active support of this subcommittee in that effort. I look forward to your questions.

Senator MURPHY. Thank you. Secretary Chollet.

STATEMENT OF HON. DEREK CHOLLET, ASSISTANT SECRETARY OF DEFENSE FOR INTERNATIONAL SECURITY AFFAIRS, U.S. DEPARTMENT OF DEFENSE, WASHINGTON, DC

Mr. CHOLLET. Thank you, Mr. Chairman and Ranking Member Johnson, for having me here today to discuss the transatlantic security challenges we face in Central and Eastern Europe, and how we are working to strengthen our allies there.

After Russia's illegal actions in Crimea, the United States took prompt steps to reassure our regional partners. First, we augmented NATO's peacetime Baltic air policing mission by sending additional fighter aircraft. Second, we deployed aircraft and personnel to Poland to supplement the U.S.-Poland Aviation Detachment, or AVDET. Third, we extended the USS *Truxtun* stay in the Black Sea to conduct exercises with Romania and Bulgaria. And fourth, we will deploy another ship next week, the USS *Donald Cook*, to the Black Sea soon to build interoperability.

NATO has dispatched AWACS platforms to fly orbits over Poland and Romania, and together with our allies, the United States wants to ensure a continuous augmented presence along NATO's borders at least through the end of the year in the air, on the ground, and at sea.

In addition to reassuring our allies, we have taken prompt action to support our NATO partner, Ukraine. The Department of Defense is working with Ukraine to review, prioritize, and grant its defense assistance request for materials and supplies. The first round of this process was completed last week with the delivery of 300,000 MREs to support Ukrainian forces who have been in the field and in need of resupply. The Ukrainians asked for this urgent assistance, and we worked hard to accommodate this request promptly.

The United States has also maintained senior level dialogues with Ukrainian counterparts throughout this crisis. Just last week, we had a senior DOD team make up of civilians and military officers in Kiev for defense talks, and this morning Secretary Hagel talked with his Ukrainian counterpart by phone. The administration is also exploring ways to support and reassure other important partners who feel threatened by Russia's actions, including Georgia and Moldova.

Mr. Chairman, Russia's illegal military action against Ukraine challenges our vision of a Europe whole, free, and at peace. And as NATO Secretary General Rasmussen said during his recent visit to Washington, ''This is the greatest threat to European security and stability since the end of the cold war.''

NATO, of course, has played a critical role. President Obama reaffirmed during his recent trip to Europe that our commitment to NATO is the most important element of U.S. national security as well as European security. And this alliance, which celebrated its 65th anniversary last week, is the organizing framework for allies to work together to manage crises. It provides an integrated military structure to support alliance political decisions to take action, and it represents our common values. Whatever other missions NATO allies agree on, collective defense, the Article 5 commitment, remains the essential glue that holds the alliance together.

Keeping NATO strong is critical to ensuring the alliance is prepared to meet the nearly continuous crises it has responded to over the past two decades. Russia's incursion into Ukraine underscores this point, and it comes at a critical time when allies are preparing for the NATO summit this September in Wales.

At this summit, allies will have to balance multiple competing issues and priorities. First, we must transition the alliance from its combat mission in Afghanistan, NATO's largest and most challenging operation ever, to the training, advice, and assist mission. Second, we must strengthen the relationship between NATO and its most capable partners who have contributed to alliance efforts in places from Libya to Afghanistan. And third, and perhaps most important, we must reenergize the political will of our allies to invest in defense capabilities. This will not only demonstrate NATO's unity and resolve, but it will also allow the alliance to meet the challenges of today and tomorrow.

Now, this goal is complicated by the evolving threat picture and the European economy crisis that has forced too many allies to cut spending, including defense investment and force structure. But the Ukraine crisis serves as a clear proof point for why we all need NATO allies to step up.

So, Mr. Chairman, Ranking Member Johnson, and members of this committee, Russia's actions in the Ukraine only reminds us of the importance of the transatlantic alliance and the benefits that comes from many years of investment to ensure that this remains strong. Now, this investment spans across administrations of both parties, and many years of bipartisan support from Congress has been indispensable.

Simply put, if NATO did not exist, we would have to invent it. So as we head toward the NATO summit this fall, we look forward to working with this committee to ensure that we are doing everything we can to strengthen the transatlantic partnership.

Thank you, and I look forward to your questions.

[The prepared statement of Mr. Chollet follows:]

PREPARED STATEMENT OF ASSISTANT SECRETARY DEREK CHOLLET

Chairman Murphy, Ranking Member Johnson, and members of the committee, thank you for inviting me here today to discuss the transatlantic security challenges we face in Central and Eastern Europe as a result of Russian actions in Ukraine. As you know, we in the Department of Defense have been preparing for this year's NATO summit, which the United Kingdom will host in Wales in September 2014. Given the Russian Federation's illegal actions in Crimea, our focus has shifted to the immediate question of how this crisis will reshape the transatlantic alliance, the upcoming summit and, more broadly speaking, NATO as a whole. My remarks today will have a two-fold focus: United States policy and actions in the short term to reassure allies and dissuade further Russian illegal use of force, and long-term implications of the recent events on our bilateral European relationships and within NATO.

REASSURING ALLIES

After Russia's illegal actions in Crimea, the United States took prompt steps to provide reassurance to NATO allies and partners in Central and Eastern Europe. We augmented NATO's peacetime Baltic Air Policing mission by deploying 6 additional F–15s. We deployed 12 F–16s and approximately 200 support personnel to Lask, Poland, to supplement the U.S.-Poland Aviation Detachment (AVDET) training rotation. We extended the USS *Truxtun*'s stay in the Black Sea through March 21 to conduct exercises with Romanian and Bulgarian naval forces, and have just ordered the USS *Donald Cook* from its new homeport in Rota, Spain, to the Black Sea to further build interoperability with allies and partners in the region.

As emphasized by President Obama in Brussels on March 26 and reinforced by Secretary of State Kerry at the April 1–2 NATO Foreign Ministerial, the United States wants to ensure a continuous, augmented presence along NATO's borders at least through the end of the year that draws on the different capabilities of NATO in the air, on the ground, and at sea to reassure our allies and demonstrate our commitment to European security. We are also assessing and updating NATO plans, and remain prepared to meet our Article 5 commitment to our NATO allies.

In addition to reassuring allies, we are also taking action to reassure Ukraine of the U.S. commitment to our partnership. On March 14, at Ukraine's request, the United States conducted an Open Skies observation mission over Ukraine territory. We are planning to send officials to Kiev to help plan a humanitarian assistance Command Post Exercise (CPX). The Department of Defense in coordination with the Department of State is working with Ukraine to review and prioritize its defense assistance requests for nonlethal materials and supplies. The first round of this process was completed last week with the delivery of 300,000 Meals Ready-to-Eat to Ukraine.

Last week, senior defense officials from the Office of the Secretary of Defense and U.S. European Command traveled to Kiev for Bilateral Defense Consultations with their Ukrainian counterparts. Although part of the discussions addressed Crimea and the buildup of Russian forces at the border, the majority of the discussion was spent on mid- and long-term bilateral defense cooperation. The U.S. Government is working with the Ukrainian Ministry of Defense to review the use of Foreign Military Financing (FMF) and International Military and Education and Training (IMET) funds based on Ukraine's new security situation, and reevaluating our mutual goals for defense institution building and professional military education in Ukraine.

Russia's actions have also increased the sense of direct threat to our other non-allied partners in Eastern Europe and the Caucasus, particularly Moldova and Georgia. The administration is already exploring ways to support these important partners. The U.S. Government has tools at its disposal to contribute to this support effort, including security assistance resources, senior leader engagement, and defense cooperation activities. Notably, senior DOD and State officials visited Moldova last week, to review with Defense Ministry officials our continuing defense cooperation, and an interagency delegation plans to visit Georgia later this month.

MAINTAINING NATO AS THE TRANSATLANTIC CORNERSTONE

Mr. Chairman, Russia's illegal military action against Ukraine challenges our vision of a Europe whole, free, and at peace. It changes Europe's security landscape, and in doing so reinforces the importance of our bilateral defense relationships with European partners and within NATO.

NATO has a critical role in regional security: it serves as the organizing framework to ensure that we have allies willing and able to fight alongside us in conflict; provides an integrated military structure to support alliance political decisions to take action; and represents our common values of democracy, individual liberty, and rule of law. NATO has evolved since the cold war to have three core missions: deterrence and collective defense; crisis management; and cooperative security. Collective defense has always been the most fundamental purpose of the alliance and is the essential glue that holds the alliance together, even during non-Article 5 operations in areas important to transatlantic security such as the Balkans and Libya. After more than a decade of out-of-area operations in Afghanistan and elsewhere, NATO will need to balance its collective security and crisis response capabilities to place more emphasis on high-end deterrence and defense while making its forces more deployable and sustainable.

Keeping NATO strong both politically and militarily is critical to ensure NATO is prepared for the nearly continuous crises it has responded to over the past 20 years, and the enduring challenges outlined at the 2012 Chicago summit: ballistic missile proliferation, cyber threats, terrorism, weapons of mass destruction, and instability from North Africa, the Middle East, and Eastern Europe. Ensuring alliance preparedness is complicated by the evolving threat picture, including Russia's activities, and the European economic crisis that is compelling allies to cut government spending, including defense investment and force structure.

While the United States must be ready to meet these emerging threats, we would prefer to meet these challenges together with allies and partners. Allies continue to look to the United States to lead the way in keeping NATO strong, capable, and credible, and President Obama has been clear on the importance of the transatlantic alliance, stating that "our commitment to NATO is the most important element of U.S. national security, as well as European security."

The September 2014 summit will occur 3 months before the transition of the NATO military mission in Afghanistan, the alliance's largest and most challenging operation in its 65 year history. The themes expected for the Wales summit include Afghanistan; the future of NATO (capabilities, training, and partnerships); and the transatlantic bond. A main summit deliverable for the United States is a successful transition from a combat mission to a train, advise, and assist mission in Afghanistan. More broadly, the United States has focused on these priorities:

- Making NATO the transatlantic core of a global security community by institutionalizing and expanding NATO's capability to build defense capacity;
- Deepening the relationship between NATO and its most capable partners; and
- Reaffirming the allies' commitment to increase defense spending and better share the burden of defense.

Mr. Chairman, Senator Johnson, and members of the committee, Russia's actions in Ukraine have required us to revisit the importance of the transatlantic alliance. The summit in Wales is an opportunity to carry forward the critical work our alliance is conducting. In Wales, we will underscore NATO's accomplishments in Afghanistan, Libya, and the Balkans—successes delivered despite financial crisis. But as we confront current challenges, most starkly demonstrated by Russia's actions, we must also invest in the future. NATO relies on individual allies for the bulk of the capabilities needed for future operations. We must find a way to ensure that NATO will be able to maintain critical capabilities in this period of austerity. We can ensure the greatness of this alliance into the next decade in spite of fiscal and security challenges, but we must invest the extra effort to work collectively and to support those institutions that facilitate our cooperation.

Senator MURPHY. Thank you to you both. I am going to start with you, Secretary Chollet, and frankly just run through three questions to ask you to respond to the three points that I made at the end of my opening statement, the first of which was a suggestion that now is the time to mount a serious defense in Congress as to why we need serious troop presence in Europe. I voted on a number of amendments when I was a Member of the House to effectively hollow out our remaining force in Europe, and of course at the time that made a lot of sense to people. Today obviously circumstances have changed.

So as you look at the troop numbers deployed throughout Europe over the course of the decade, understanding that sequestration is still a reality, what are DOD's thoughts?

Mr. CHOLLET. Mr. Chairman, as you noted in your opening statement, Secretary Hagel said a few days ago that what we are looking at is our troop presence in Europe. It has gone down significantly, as you know, over the last two decades. We have got about 57,000 or so troops permanently stationed in Europe.

And General Breedlove, the SACEUR and EUCOM commander, was tasked just last week to come up with some further reassurance steps we may take with our European partners to help reassure our Central and European allies that this would not be just unilateral U.S. steps, but steps that we would take as members of the NATO alliance. And he will be reporting on some of that planning next week, and we will be working through then the NATO alliance.

So whereas I do not foresee major changes in our permanent footprint in Europe, I think that what we are trying to explore are ways that we can leverage some of these rotational deployments that we have undertaken, for example, the Poland Aviation Detachment, which is a relatively modest investment, and it is a very small permanent footprint, but it is very significant for our Polish partners transitioning through F–16s or C–130s to help with their training.

And ways we can augment and build on that, I think, is a way that we can have a forward presence, work closely with our partners, and help build their capabilities. But it will also, very importantly, be efficient in these austere budget times.

Senator MURPHY. Poland has requested for two NATO brigades. What is the Department of Defense's position on that request?

Mr. CHOLLET. So that is something that General Breedlove is working through, and so we will wait his assessment.

Senator MURPHY. The second point that I initially made was regarding military sales with Russia. You know, it is difficult to understand how the French could continue to sell ships to Russia that are identical to the ones that were used in the illegal invasion and occupation of Crimea. Do we think that our European allies are serious about ending military relationships or curtailing military relationships with Russia in the wake of this crisis?

Mr. CHOLLET. Well, Senator, it is something we have very frank conversations with our European colleagues about. You mentioned also suspending arms sales to Russia overall and sectorial sanctions, which the President has signed an Executive order giving himself the authority to do. Those are the sorts of things we would consider. We have not done that yet, but we have the authority to do so. And the Department of Defense, the Department of State across our government have had very frank conversations, again, with our French colleagues, in particular, about the way forward and their relationship with Russia.

Senator MURPHY. I will ask this one first to you, Secretary Chollet, but then toss it to Secretary Nuland as well, and that is to ask for a little bit more color on what you believe to be a successful Wales summit. I think you actually laid out three principles. But let me ask you specifically with respect to the question of enlargement.

I understand the position that Georgia is in. I know that they have some serious steps still to be taken before they are a candidate for full admission into NATO. But a membership action plan can have lots of steps and caveats and hoops to jump through. It would seem to be a very strong signal to both Russia and to our allies that we are serious about keeping the open door policy in NATO if we were to give a MAP to Georgia. I know there are other countries that are interested in getting that status at Wales, but if you could both comment perhaps generally on the issue of enlargement and then specifically to Georgia.

Mr. CHOLLET. So, Senator, I will take the first answer, and then turn it over to Victoria. The door remains open. It is something we strongly support. And in the specific case of Georgia, we very much support Georgia's Euro-Atlantic orientation and ambitions. Georgia, from a DOD perspective, U.S. Government as a whole perspective, Georgia is a terrific partner. They were in the fight with us in Afghanistan without caveats, taking risks. They have committed to remain with us post-2014 in Afghanistan, and so they are a very strong partner.

We, the United States, are supportive of the membership action plan, and we have expressed that. But as you know very well, this is an alliance decision. It is not a decision the United States will make alone. So we work closely with our Georgian partners through this process, and it something that clearly will be a subject of conversation in the months ahead as we lead up to the Wales summit.

Senator MURPHY. Secretary Nuland.

Ms. NULAND. Well, as ever, Derek has articulated beautifully. Just to say that the Georgians are well aware that they do not have consensus in the alliance, and that they have work to do to convince particularly some of our Western European allies of their worthiness for the membership action plan. We have been supporting them as they make this case directly to individual allies.

One thing that happens very soon for Georgia is it is on track to sign its association agreement with the European Union, which will deepen its relationship with many of these same countries. So we are hopeful that that will have a positive impact on how they assess its worthiness from that.

Senator MURPHY. I am going to stay outside Ukraine and maybe use a quick second round to talk about Ukraine. Secretary Nuland, you were just in Moldova, and I know that Senator Johnson is going to be there, so maybe I am preempting a question from him. But as we try to perhaps learn from the things that we could have done or that the alliance could have done in Ukraine in the months and years leading up to this crisis, which I am not suggesting anyone could have foreseen, what do you think are the most important steps to strengthen the transatlantic alliance with Moldova to send the right message to Russia and to perhaps prepare them for the potential of some kind of offensive action from Russia and Transnistria?

Ms. NULAND. Well, thank you, Senator. As you know, we have intensified our collaboration and cooperation with Moldova. Secretary Kerry was there in December. As you said, I was there again a week ago Sunday.

Our primary effort with Moldova has been to support their preparations for an association agreement signing with the EU and the deep and comprehensive free trade agreement, because both of these will strengthen their trade, and travel, and links to Europe, and give them more options than simply the Russian market. We are also working intensively with them on energy security and alternative sources. We are investing with the European Union in interconnectors with Romania.

We are also helping them diversify their trade market. They are trying to import some of their spectacular wine, which I hope will sample, Senator Johnson, when you are there, into the United States. And we have linked them up with a number of key U.S. distributors. We are also helping—they have a Millennium Challenge Compact, as you know, which supports bringing agriculture to market, road and water support.

So we are doing all those things, but also supporting their path to elections as well. In the fall, a very important set of elections for them. So it is a key moment.

We are also trying to help them. One of the things that was somewhat distressing on my last trip was whereas there was very strong support within Moldova for the association agreement and for tighter links with Europe, the Russian propaganda effort has been particularly virulent across the country, but especially in the Russian-speaking areas. And the Moldovan Government and the EU frankly have not done a strong enough job of explaining the benefits, what it is going to feel like when citizens across the country in just a few months can have visa-free travel to Europe, can have tariff-free export for the goods, including the goods of many of these factories in Transnistria. So this is a job that needs more attention, and we are going to put some more effort into it ourselves.

Senator MURPHY. Well, I appreciate that answer. I will turn it over to Senator Johnson, but I hope that our friends in Brussels heard your answer to that last question. There is nothing untoward about advertising yourself. And we know that the Russians do not play by the same rules that we do. But the fact is that in Moldova today, as you maintain, there is a battle for the hearts and minds of the people there as to whether they are going to orient toward Europe or back toward Russia. And the fact is that the EU is not doing a good enough job in Moldova, nor did they do a good enough job in parts of Ukraine explaining what the true benefits of that alliance are, while the entire time the Russians are investing all sorts of clean and dirty money in an effort to tell a very different story.

There is a propaganda war being fought. There is only one side right now that is truly at a high level fighting it. And we can certainly be partners in that, but ultimately this is not a matter of the United States convincing people in Moldova whether they should or should not join the European Union. It is really up to the European Union.

Senator Johnson.

Senator JOHNSON. Thank you, Mr. Chairman. Let me pick up right there in terms of the propaganda war. I agree it is basically one-sided, so let me go to you, Secretary Nuland. Are we doing anything to provide the alternate view and try and provide information now into Moldova, but also into Ukraine and the other Baltic States?

Ms. NULAND. Thanks for that, Senator. This has been a major line of effort led by Secretary Kerry, but very much supported by the President as well, over the last 2 months to—you know, one cannot match the kind of money and effort in a closed society that Russia is putting into this. But we can certainly help our friends and partners debunk lies, get the straight story out.

So we have redirected a great amount of public diplomacy funds to mounting our own truth-telling campaign, which we are pushing out in Ukrainian, in Russian, in all of the European languages, but also in English across the United States and across allied territory.

We have a number of products that we have mounted—the United for Ukraine campaign on Twitter. If you are not linked up to that, please link up. That was started at the State Department and now has many thousands of users and repeat tweeters. We have a product called the Daily Playbook where twice, three times a week, sometimes daily we put out all of the positive news about what is happening in Ukraine, and we also debunk falsehoods from the Russian Federation, including this most recent one where they accused a United States company of having mercenaries across Ukraine. And when we called the company, they made absolutely clear that no such thing was true, and this was something that was put out on the Foreign Ministry Web site. So this kind of thing.

So we are doing a lot. We have put an additional $3.3 million into support for the Ukrainian Government itself, and I said, we are going to redirect some money to Moldova as well.

Senator JOHNSON. What about broadcast medium—TV, radio? It came to our attention there was apparently a TV station with an uplink that could have broadcast into Russia that was for sale that could have been purchased. Is there any effort—any expenditures being made to widen our ability to broadcast?

Ms. NULAND. Well, we are supporting Ukrainian broadcasting companies that are broadcasting in both Russian and Ukrainian. We are also supporting the media center that the transitional government has set up to help them exploit available opportunities for broadcasting. We have RFERL, which is very active in this space in all of its languages. We have not looked into buying TV ourselves. I am not sure that is the best use of resources. Rather we are trying to partner with folks in Ukraine and in Europe who are active in this space.

Senator JOHNSON. Okay. Secretary Chollet, first of all, congratulations on the new addition to your family. You mentioned that Secretary Hagel had talked to defense officials in Ukraine. Can you tell me what that conversation was about?

Mr. CHOLLET. Sir, he has had many conversations over the last several months with his Ukrainian counterparts. I should stress ''counterparts'' because there has been—I think this is the fourth defense minister he has talked to in the last several months. And this is mainly to ensure that we have at the highest level a channel of communication throughout this crisis and so we can hear from them directly about their needs and about ways that we may be able to help then.

Senator JOHNSON. Are they specifying needs?

Mr. CHOLLET. Yes and no. I mean, the Ukrainian military was not an extraordinarily capable military before this crisis, and it has been, as I mentioned in my opening statement, been in the field, deployed, and been under quite significant hardship over the last several weeks given Russia's behavior. So the most urgent needs that they have identified to us have been in the more nonlethal humanitarian spaces, the MREs and medical supplies in particular. So we are working to try to accommodate those requests.

Senator JOHNSON. When Prime Minister Yatsenyuk was here, I know he made a request for some small arms and ammunition, which was apparently turned down. Part of the rationale was we certainly did not want to do anything that could provoke Vladimir Putin. Now, this was before the vote. This was before the annexation. Guess he did not need any provocation. He just did it anyway.

Are we rethinking our willingness to help Ukraine militarily from the standpoint of supplying them the types of small arms and ammunition they requested back then?

Mr. CHOLLET. Well, Senator, we are constantly in a dialogue with them about what they may need. This team that was in Kiev last week were discussions that were already planned.

Senator JOHNSON. That is great. Dialogue is great. Are we rethinking whether or not we are going to provide them the type of support they actually requested and they actually need if Vladimir Putin moves further?

Mr. CHOLLET. Yes, but the priority right now is—their own prioritization that they presented to us is mainly nonlethal at this point. But as we are looking out at this immediate crisis that we are in and thinking of the medium and the long term, which is what we talked about last week in Kiev, is as they are seeking to further modernize their military, and they are seeking to further professionalize their military—by the way, efforts that we have tried to work very closely with them on in the last several years, long before this crisis. And they still have a long way to go on professionalization and modernization, ways that we can be helpful.

Senator JOHNSON. You mentioned that NATO is augmenting their presence along the borders. What does ''augmentation'' mean? How many personnel are we talking about?

Mr. CHOLLET. So we could get you the exact numbers of total NATO personnel.

I can tell you from a United States perspective, for example, in Poland the aviation detachment and the upgrade by adding some aircraft to that attachment, I think a couple hundred folks have accompanied that. Similar with the Baltic air policing mission and our augmenting of that effort, it is a handful of folks. And part of what General Breedlove will be coming back to NATO and briefing next week is his proposal for the over the medium to the long term for the rest of this how whether by air, land, and sea, NATO, the United States, and our other 27 allies, can be postured differently, and particularly in Central and Eastern Europe in response to the crisis.

Senator JOHNSON. So currently our response to the Russian troop buildup of tens of thousands—it is hard to say what the exact number is—but tens of thousands of Russian troop buildup along the eastern border of Ukraine is a couple of hundred and dozens? Do you really think that is going to change Vladimir Putin's calculation?

Mr. CHOLLET. Well, sir, I think what is most likely to change his calculation is what we have been seeking as a government, not the Department of Defense, but mainly with our colleagues at Treasury on sanctions and hitting the Russian government where it really matters.

Senator JOHNSON. Is it not true that Russian officials mocked the sanctions?

Mr. CHOLLET. Well, as Secretary Kerry said before this committee a few days ago, initially there was some chatter and mocking, but I think that these sanctions pinch. They hurt. There is no doubt. And as the President made very clear when he announced this latest round of sanctions, it is not the limit of what we can do. There are further things we can do. But as is clear, the further we go, the greater ramifications it could also have on us.

That said, we have made very clear to the Russian Government that we stand by our Article 5 commitment to NATO allies, that their behavior is unacceptable, and that we are rethinking many things when it comes to our military posture in Europe.

Senator JOHNSON. Okay. Thank you.

Senator MURPHY. I am just going to take time for a short second round here. I would just in general associate myself with the remarks of Senator Johnson. I think we are beyond the point of treading lightly. I think we are beyond the point of worrying about provoking Russia. I think that they are going to make decisions about the future course of events in and around Ukraine based on their own security needs.

And as one neighbor of Russia around the Black Sea came and told Senator Johnson and me earlier this week, that our response should be to do everything that Russia does not want us to do. And while I have expressed skepticism about providing small arms, I think a successful NATO summit with an extension of a membership action plan to Georgia and continued ratcheting up of sanctions is exactly that medicine.

Two questions, one for you, Secretary Nuland. Can you just give an update on the elections schedule for May 25? Maybe give us a sense of—you know, I do not want you to be apocalyptic, but what is Russia's capability to undermine these elections when today they do not have a candidate that at least is polling at any level that would suggest they are a true threat?

So what do we worry about, and what are the things that we and our Ukrainian allies can do to make sure that Ukrainians get a choice, because if they have a free and fair election, there is no way the next President and the next Cabinet of Ukraine is going to give the time of day to Putin in the next administration.

Ms. NULAND. Well, thanks, Senator. First of all, as you may have seen, there are more than 20 candidates registered for the Presidential election on May 25 representing every single available color of the political spectrum in Ukraine. So the Ukrainian people will certainly have a very broad choice, and the election is likely to throw to a runoff, which is a very, very healthy thing.

The media environment, the basic conditions for this election at this moment, absent the security situation, are as good as they have ever been in Ukraine with a very, very supportive transitional national government, with a very supportive Rada, with a vibrant public debate going on public media and private media.

The other thing is we have a very strong response from the OSCE from ODIHR. They are planning to field more than a thousand monitors across the country. The Ukrainians are also making provisions for Crimeans to vote. They will not be able to vote in Crimea because Russia will not allow it, but there will be polling places for them.

And as I understand it, I testified before the Helsinki Commission yesterday, and we will have a big contingent as well. We have an NDI and IRI contingent under Helsinki. So that is a part of the answer to have eyes all over this process so that it cannot be manipulated. But the number one concern we have now is efforts to destabilize the eastern regions, other parts of Ukraine, to create either a pretext for declaring it too difficult to have elections, to create questions about it, and/or for a larger Russian move into Ukraine to protect citizens.

So this is the real threat that these moves in Kharkhiv, Donetsk, and Luhansk pose. The interesting thing is that none of this has any kind of significant support among the populations, including the populations of the east. There was recent IRI polling and there is recent Ukrainian polling indicating than less than 15 percent of those in the east want to join Russia. They want to stay in a united Ukraine. They want to have a choice of their future.

There are candidates, as I said, across the spectrum for people to vote for, including those who want a closer relationship with Russia, but not to hive off pieces of Ukraine or allow the kind of federalization that could cause the country to fall apart. So I think you are going to see a very, very vibrant debate, but the number one risk is the security situation and this aggressive effort with an address back to Moscow to destabilize.

Senator MURPHY. And, of course, the irony is the more successful we are making sure that that election is free and fair, the more worried we have to be about Russia's intentions once they see the writing on the wall.

One question for you, Secretary Chollet, back to United States military support for Ukraine. It seems to me that one of the logical programs that we could undertake, whether it is the United States or with NATO, is a longer term project to rebuild the strength of the Ukrainian Armed Forces. They were obviously hollowed out under Yanukovych and probably even prior to that. And separate and aside from the decisions that you make about their immediate needs, what about a long-term commitment to help them rebuild their military?

Mr. CHOLLET. Senator, absolutely agree. That kind of long-term thinking was what we had embarked upon long before this crisis, and I think that this crisis provides an opportunity for us to think anew about how we can continue the efforts we had started, but really augment them further.

Our military relationship with Ukraine, although important, and they deployed with us in Afghanistan and elsewhere was relatively modest. It is $4 million or so a year in FMF. So part of these discussions that we were having in Kiev last week was about the medium to long term and how we can address their urgent needs, but more importantly perhaps over the long term ensure that they continue on the modernization and professionalization effort that we have helped with.

Senator MURPHY. I think the noisier we are about that longer term commitment, the better.

Senator Johnson.

Senator JOHNSON. I have been concerned. I have been hearing a term, "Finlandization." I have heard things like "redlines around Ukraine." Is that something that our NATO partners or that we—are we using those terms in any way, shape, or form?

Ms. NULAND. Senator, we are not. That term has different meanings to different people, but it generally implies a constitutional neutrality of one kind of or another. As you know, the transitional government in Ukraine, and you have probably heard this from Prime Minister Yatsenyuk, has said that they do not have any plans while they are in power to change the "nonbloc status of the country." But obviously it is a matter for future leaders of Ukrain and the Ukrainian people to decide how they might want to associate in the future. It is not a decision that the United States or any other country can make for Ukraine or for Ukrainians.

Senator JOHNSON. So we are standing by the assurance that we basically granted by being a signatory to the Budapest memorandum to do everything we can to maintain the border integrity of Ukraine.

Ms. NULAND. Well, as you know, that was signed in 1994 as a political assurance that we would all support and defend the sovereignty and territorial integrity of Ukraine. It did not have the status of a treaty commitment, and as such has been brutally violated by the Russian Federation. Of course, our own commitment remains solid, but Russia did not have any trouble trampling on that.

Senator, if I may, can I just go back to your point about whether sanctions are biting? You know, it is easy is if you are sitting in Moscow to mock them, but the numbers tell a different story. More than $25 billion spent by the Russia Federation over the last 5 to 6 weeks to prop up the ruble to defend it. Some capital flight in the first quarter of 2014 out of Russia, greater than capital flight throughout all of 2013, which was a significant year for capital flight from Russia. A great shrinking economy. It was already shrinking. It is shrinking even more. Downgrading of Russia by the major rating organizations. So this is pinching, but you are not wrong that we have to maintain the pressure.

Senator JOHNSON. Okay. Thank you very much.

Senator MURPHY. Thank you to both of our witnesses. We really appreciate your time and our late start. You are dismissed, and as you leave we will seat our second panel. Thank you very much to both of our Secretaries.

[Pause.]

Senator MURPHY. Let me welcome our second panel with one caveat. Senator Cardin is on his way and will be taking over the chairmanship of this portion of the hearing in about 20 minutes or so. I unfortunately have another obligation, and we are going to try to wrap this up as quickly as we can given what is happening on the floor.

But we are very excited to have our guests today. Julianne Smith is a senior fellow and director of the Strategy and Statecraft Program at the Center for a New American Security, and a senior vice president at Beacon Global Strategies. She previously served as the Deputy National Security Adviser to Vice President Biden and the Principal Director for Europe and NATO policy in the Office of the Secretary of Defense.

Ian Brzezinski is a senior fellow with the Brent Scowcroft Center on International Security at the Atlantic Council. He brings more than two decades of experience in U.S. national security, including serving as Deputy Assistant Secretary of Defense for Europe and NATO policy.

And Edward Chow is a senior fellow in the Energy and National Security Program at the Center for Strategic and International Studies. Before coming to CSIS, he spent 30 years working in the energy industry, including 20 years with the Chevron Corporation.

Welcome to all of you. We will go in the order that I introduced to you from Ms. Smith to Mr. Brzezinski to Mr. Chow.

STATEMENT OF JULIANNE SMITH, DIRECTOR, STRATEGY AND STATECRAFT PROGRAM, CENTER FOR A NEW AMERICAN SECURITY, WASHINGTON, DC

Ms. SMITH. Well, thank you very much, Chairman Murphy, Ranking Member Johnson. Thank you for the opportunity to testify today on transatlantic security challenges.

As you well know, Russia's recent annexation of Crimea obviously has raised a lot of thorny questions about the future of transatlantic security. Europe and the United States, as you heard earlier from Secretary Chollet and Secretary Nuland, share three common objectives associated with this crisis. One is obviously isolating Russia and ensuring that there are additional costs imposed on the Russians. Two is reassuring our allies in Central and Eastern Europe. And the third is supporting the new interim government in Kiev.

I am going to take the first two, and I want to start with reassuring our allies in Central and Eastern Europe. You heard earlier from Assistant Secretary Chollet about some of the things that the United States was able to do in the early days of the crisis from providing additional F–15s to the Baltic States and F–16s to Poland to extending the stay of the USS *Truxtun,* in the Black Sea to other plans that we have for the region to reassure our skittish allies.

Europe, Western European in particular, was slower to respond to this crisis and to calls for reassurance from our allies in Central and Eastern Europe. They have had a number of concerns about unnecessarily provoking the Russians. They have looked at public opinion data, which frankly does not support initiatives that would reassure our friends in Central and Eastern Europe. And some of them, frankly, lack the sheer capability to do so.

Now, some of that has changed. We had a NATO ministerial a couple of weeks ago, and we saw a number of Western European countries step forward and offer forms of support to Central and Eastern Europe. And as you heard, General Breedlove will be presenting some other options on Tuesday that I hope will be supported not just by the United States, but by the alliance as a whole.

Moving forward, I think the challenge for Europe and the United States is to keep the momentum going and get to a point where we do not allow our policy differences to lead to policy paralysis. We do not want to find ourselves in the situation where we are breeding additional overconfidence on the part of the Russians, or allowing the Russians to drive a wedge right through the middle of NATO.

And in my written testimony, which I have submitted for the record today, I suggest three things that Europe and the United States should be focused on. The first one is to present a united front even when sometimes we cannot reach consensus. You know better than I do that there are some cracks in the transatlantic relationship on this issue. At times, we have disagreed. In the early days of the crisis, we had some public airing of our differences, particularly over sanctions, which I think was not a wise move on both of our parts.

I think as we disagree and we weigh the pros and cons of additional initiatives moving forward, we have to ensure that we keep what is actually at stake in the back of our minds and remember that Crimea is not a bump in the road. This is not a hiccup. This is not a short-term incident. What happened in Crimea will have lasting implications for transatlantic security and for the region as a whole. In my mind, we are not going back to business as usual, and so it is important to keep that in mind as we think about a long-term strategy that would include economic, diplomatic, and military measures.

The second thing, I think what we have to focus on as allies is getting the NATO piece right. You heard from Assistant Secretary Chollet and Assistant Secretary Nuland that there is a NATO summit coming up, of course, in the fall. We are going to need U.S. leadership to drive some of those initiatives forward on some very difficult issues. You mentioned, Chairman, NATO enlargement as one issue. You are well aware of the differences inside the alliance on that particular issue.

But if we do not take on NATO enlargement, if we do not take on cyber, if we do not take on missile defense, if we do not take on some of these tough issues, I think NATO will ultimately be unprepared to deal with what is coming at it in the 21st century and beyond, not just with this crisis, but with others.

The Secretary General of NATO has been very optimistic in recent days saying that Ukraine is a game changer and will hopefully lead to increases in defense spending. I am not so sure, but I would like to count on Washington's leadership to drive that debate forward. And also managing the debate we have had many times about Article 5 versus expeditionary operations.

The last thing that I think Europe and the United States need to focus on is making sure that they do not leave a gray zone between NATO territory and Ukraine. We need to look at the reassurance requirements not just in countries like Poland and the Baltic States, but also Georgia and Moldova.

In many ways, these countries need more assurance than those that are already members of NATO and the EU, and so, we will have to look at things like defense cooperation and security cooperation. We are going to have to put everything on the table to ensure that there is a united front between Europe and the United States. It just cannot be the United States alone.

In terms of our efforts—Europe and European efforts—to support the new team in Ukraine, we are trying to support the elections as we talked about earlier. We are working to provide them financial assistance so that their economy does not collapse, and we are trying to address their security needs simultaneously.

I think we have done all right in the first two categories. We are trying to ensure that they have the tools they need for a free and fair election. We have provided billions of dollars and promises of loan assistance, and all sorts of technical expertise.

But I think we have not done particularly well in addressing the security concerns. I know you heard a moment ago that DOD is looking at some of those requests, but we have had the good fortune to date of relying on incredible restraint on the part of the Ukrainian military. I do not think we can count on that in the long term. We are not so sure how much longer we will see such restraint, particularly given some of the protests we have seen in eastern Ukraine.

And so, I think moving forward, the United States is going to have to ramp up its efforts to review those requests, nonlethal and lethal, and determine if we can provide additional intel-sharing, training, and look at things like ammunition.

To close, I just want to say I think Europe and the United States deserve kudos and credit for the work that they have done together in multiple categories of addressing different aspects of this crisis. But what they have done to date should really be seen as the opening act. I think we have to sustain this momentum, make sure we have a long-term strategy, and make sure that that strategy is paired with real resources and real capabilities.

We also have to think through the potential scenarios that we might be facing in the future. What happens if Russia goes into eastern Ukraine? What happens if the Russians try to further destabilize Transnistria? Or what happens if those May 25 elections do not happen? We need to be having that kind of conversation with our European allies now to prepare ourselves for anything that might be coming down the road.

Thank you very much, and I look forward to your questions.

[The prepared statement of Ms. Smith follows:]

PREPARED STATEMENT OF JULIANNE SMITH

Chairman Murphy, Ranking Member Johnson, and distinguished members of the subcommittee, thank you for the opportunity to testify today on the transatlantic security challenges in Central and Eastern Europe. I appreciate the subcommittee's attention to this issue—one that I have written about as a scholar and focused on closely while serving in the Obama administration.

Russia's recent annexation of Crimea raises a number of questions about the future of transatlantic security. Europe and the United States share three core objectives associated with this crisis all of which require close transatlantic cooperation: isolating Russia and halting further Russian aggression, reassuring allies in Central and Eastern Europe and supporting the interim government in Kiev. I would like to focus today on the last two tasks. Both sides of the Atlantic deserve praise for their ongoing work in these areas but several challenges lie ahead. It will be absolutely critical in the coming weeks and months for the transatlantic partners to show continuing resolve, enhance their efforts to date and ensure that they don't provide President Putin with an opportunity to drive a wedge through NATO or the transatlantic relationship more broadly.

TRANSATLANTIC EFFORTS TO REASSURE CENTRAL AND EASTERN EUROPE

The countries of Central and Eastern Europe have watched events in Ukraine with considerable alarm. Given their proximity to Russia's borders; their inability to counter a Russian military threat relying solely on their own defense forces; past experience with various types of Russian intimidation; and, in some cases, Russian minorities numbering in the hundreds of thousands (which could potentially serve as a pretext for Russian aggression), many of the countries in this region are feeling increasingly vulnerable. Even NATO member states that benefit from an Article 5 security guarantee and countries like Poland that have made considerable progress in modernizing their own defense forces over the last 20 years have made it clear in recent weeks that they are seeking additional layers of reassurance from both sides of the Atlantic.

In the first few days following the Crimea crisis, the United States undertook a number of steps to address the security concerns of its NATO allies in Central and Eastern Europe. Those steps included dispatching six F–15s to the Baltic States as part of the ongoing Baltic Air Policing Mission, extending the USS *Truxtun*'s stay in the Black Sea and deploying 12 F–16s and 200 airmen to Poland. The United States also plans to send F–16 fighter jets to Romania this month as part of planned joint exercises, and a guided missile destroyer is scheduled to arrive in the Black Sea today for training and exercises.

In comparison to the United States, Western Europe was somewhat slower to respond to reassurance requests stemming from Central and Eastern Europe. Some countries like the United Kingdom and France offered swift support and NATO agreed in mid-March to send two surveillance planes to fly over Poland and Romania. But a number of countries in Western Europe felt that NATO's security guarantee should be sufficient and were hesitant to commit to do more either due to resourcing constraints or concerns about unnecessarily provoking the Russians. There are signs, however, that European reticence is changing. NATO's recent ministerial in Brussels on April 1–2 succeeded in garnering additional forms of support for Central and Eastern Europe. At least eight countries pledged to provide assets to bolster the NATO's eastern flank.[1] NATO's supreme military commander, Gen. Philip Breedlove, was tasked to look for additional ways to deploy or reinforce land, sea and air forces in Eastern Europe, upgrade training and military exercises and update contingency plans. In addition, NATO foreign ministers discussed ways in which they might boost the readiness of the NATO Response Force (NRF) consisting of 13,000 troops available on short notice.

CEE allies, while appreciative of these steps, continue to yearn for tangible measures beyond reassurance especially in light of the recent protests in eastern Ukraine, which by many accounts are being orchestrated by Russia and could serve as a pretext for more Russian aggression. Specifically, some countries such as Poland and the Baltic States have made it clear that what they really want is a permanent ground presence. At the NATO Ministerial in early April, Radek Sikorski, the Polish Foreign Minister, asked NATO to station 10,000 troops on Polish territory as a demonstration of NATO's resolve to defend its member states. That request went unanswered but raised one of the toughest questions associated with reassuring NATO allies in Central and Eastern Europe —will the alliance consider abandoning a 1997 pledge to Russia not to permanently station NATO troops in new member states?[2] That question has triggered a lively debate inside the halls of NATO and across the capitals of NATO member states.

While a number of European countries have condemned the Russian annexation of Crimea in the harshest terms and called for punitive measures, few Western European leaders have shown a willingness to date to reverse the 1997 pledge not to station troops in Eastern Europe. When he was asked at the NATO Ministerial about this issue, the Dutch Foreign Minister, Frans Timmermanns, responded by stating, "No, we don't need any NATO troops on the border with Russia."[3] That sentiment has been repeated by officials in Berlin and other European capitals.[4] The rationale behind it is multifold. First and foremost, a number of NATO members worry about the risks of escalating the conflict with Russia at a time when they are pursuing diplomatic means to solve the crisis. Second, publics in some NATO member states oppose even less controversial reassurance measures in Central and Eastern European. For example, in Germany, more than 60 percent of the population opposes sending the country's air force to strengthen NATO's eastern borders (which would not be inconsistent with the 1997 pledge).[5] Finally, as they prepare to withdraw from over a decade of conflict in Afghanistan, some NATO members simply lack the will to deploy ground forces. Others just lack the actual capabilities to do so. All that said, NATO should immediately determine if Russia has already broken its own promises outlined in the NATO-Russia Founding Act, thereby freeing us of the 1997 obligation and opening up the option of stationing troops in Eastern Europe.

While the United States has yet to respond formally to Poland's request for ground troops, Secretary Hagel, during a meeting with Asian defense ministers in Hawaii on April 3, indicated that the U.S. was looking at the possibility of permanently stationing an additional U.S. Army brigade in Europe. Considering that it was just a little more than 2 years ago when the Department of Defense withdrew from Europe two of its four Army brigades and eliminated them from the force, doing so would represent a substantial reversal in U.S. force posture. It is no secret that the United States is facing genuine resource constraints that have forced the administration to prioritize its core missions, shrink the size of its armed forces and reduce its global presence. As a result, any additional U.S. commitment in Eastern Europe will have to be weighed against competing defense priorities. If permanently stationing troops in Eastern Europe proves to be a bridge too far, the United States should at least consider earmarking another U.S.-based Brigade Combat Team (BCT) for rotation in Europe.

The core challenge for the transatlantic partners will be to prevent their differences on the ground forces request and other related issues from leading to policy paralysis that would only boost Putin's confidence and unnerve skittish NATO allies in Central and Eastern Europe. Looking ahead, Europe and the United States should focus on the following:

Present a united front even when there isn't consensus. It is clear that there are already cracks in transatlantic cooperation, particularly in regard to reassuring allies in Central and Eastern Europe. When that happens, it is important that the two sides of the Atlantic avoid airing their differences in public (as they did on the utility of sanctions during the first few days of the crisis), which gives Moscow the satisfaction of feeling like it has the upper hand. As Europe and the United States look at additional measures to pursue in Central and Eastern Europe, in Ukraine or vis-a-vis Russia, they must keep in mind what is at stake and what lessons other corners of the world might draw from their perceived inaction or indecisiveness. The Ukraine crisis is not a short-term hiccup in our relationship with Russia but a wake-up call about the importance of transatlantic unity and resolve in the long term. This crisis will require additional measures using a wide variety of economic, diplomatic, and military tools, which at times will test the transatlantic partners both economically and politically (especially as they begin to look at ways to reduce Europe's reliance on Russian oil and gas). Accepting and committing to that reality is an important first step.

Get the NATO piece right. NATO Secretary General Anders Fogh Rasmussn has repeatedly stressed that the Ukraine crisis will serve as a ''game changer'' for the alliance, one that will return it to its core mission of collective defense. He has also expressed his hope that the crisis will spur NATO members to spend more on defense after decades of defense cuts that have hollowed out NATO capabilities. While that optimistic vision has been welcomed in Washington and a handful of other NATO member states particularly in Central and Eastern Europe, much more work needs to be done to build consensus on the way ahead. Not all members see Ukraine as a turning point. Not all members are prepared to put collective defense above NATO's other focus on expeditionary operations. Not all members feel compelled to develop new reassurance and deterrence initiatives to ensure that Russia doesn't get any ideas about moving toward NATO member states. That is especially true in regard to the upcoming NATO summit in the United Kingdom this September. That summit currently revolves around three main baskets of work: the end of the alliance's combat mission in Afghanistan, a new transatlantic compact and the future of NATO partnerships. It is hard to imagine Ukraine not having a major impact on the last two baskets. The question of course is how and to what degree. Some members, again due to resource constraints or interest in avoiding confrontation with the Russians, will no doubt opt for mere symbolic gestures. But the United States, in tandem with the Secretary General, will need to lead the effort to develop robust initiatives that showcase NATO's resolve, innovation, and unity. That means taking on the highly sensitive subjects of NATO enlargement, cyber security, energy security and missile defense. The United States will also have to take a leadership role in navigating what will no doubt be a rigorous but dated debate over Article 5 missions vs. expeditionary operations.

Don't forget those countries in the region that are not NATO members. Europe and the United States have largely focused reassurance efforts on current NATO members and Ukraine. But they will need to keep their eye on those countries that sit just outside of NATO territory—countries like Georgia and Moldova that are in many ways more vulnerable than their neighbors that are already in NATO and the EU. Understandably, these countries are also seeking visible signs of reassurance (preferably via military channels) as well as political and economic assistance. Given that the collective weight of Europe and the United States far surpasses anything that either side of the Atlantic might do unilaterally, transatlantic coordination will be an indispensible part of any European or American initiative in this regard. A U.S. Assistant Secretary of State and a Deputy Assistant Secretary of Defense recently traveled together to Moldova to review U.S. defense cooperation. Europe should follow suit and work with Washington to develop joint initiatives so that the two sides of the Atlantic don't inadvertently leave a gray zone between NATO territory and Ukraine.

TRANSATLANTIC EFFORTS TO SUPPORT UKRAINE

In addition to reassuring allies in Central and Eastern Europe, Europe and the United States have sought ways to assist the interim government of Ukraine, which faces three enormous tasks: prevent the Ukrainian economy from collapsing, prepare for May elections and avoid a military confrontation with Russia, particularly in eastern Ukraine, which is looking increasingly unstable. While the two partners deserve relatively high marks in the first two categories, little has been done to assist in the last.

Ukraine estimates that it will need upward of $35 billion in foreign assistance over the next 2 years to avert default.[6] To their credit, both the European Union (EU) and the United States came forward with pledges of assistance ($15 billion and $1 billion respectively) shortly after the crisis began. The EU and Ukraine also recently signed the political chapters of the Association Agreement, committing them to closer political and economic cooperation. In late March the IMF stepped forward with an agreement to provide $18 billion in loans over the next 2 years. On top of all of this important financial assistance, both sides of the Atlantic have sent, or will soon send, a number of policy experts, high-ranking policymakers, and business delegations to offer technical assistance and much-needed reassurance.

As with their joint efforts to reassure the countries of Central and Eastern Europe, the transatlantic partners will have to avoid a situation where support drops off once Ukraine falls off the front pages of the world's newspapers (assuming it actually does). Getting Ukraine on the healthy path of stability and prosperity will takes years, if not decades, of work and billions of dollars, a fact that neither side of the Atlantic can afford to underestimate. Of course, the risks and rewards could not be clearer. If Ukraine succeeds in reforming its economy, it could serve as an important beacon of hope for others in the region and refute the Russian notion that countries in Russia's neighborhood do not have the freedom to choose their own future. If it fails, however, it could "become a huge festering sore on Europe's frontiers, capable of undermining the political health of the entire region, including the eastern reaches of the EU itself."[7]

In regard to the upcoming elections, the United States and Europe must do everything they can to assist the interim government of Ukraine prepare for its May 25 election. As Secretary Kerry noted in his testimony yesterday, no one in Kiev has revealed any plans to delay these elections. As partners, Europe and the United States must ensure it stays that way. The two sides of the Atlantic will need to deploy international election monitors and provide Kiev with the tools they need to ensure free and fair elections, which will be an important step forward on the road to economic and political recovery.

As for the task of supporting the interim government in Ukraine as it copes with an immediate Russian military threat on its border, only modest steps have been taken by the United States and Europe to date. Washington sent Deputy Assistant Secretary of Defense Evelyn Farkas to Kiev to represent Secretary Hagel during Bilateral Defense Consultations with the Ukrainian Government. That was a good start to a conversation about Ukraine's short- to medium-term military requirements but it should ultimately lead to U.S. plans to meet at least some of those requirements. The United States is also looking at International Military and Education and Training as well as Foreign Military Financing.

NATO is moving forward with its upcoming military exercise in Ukraine this summer called Rapid Trident, which will bring together over a thousand international forces. The alliance has expressed its willingness to intensify its military cooperation with Ukraine, including assisting in modernizing its military. Individual European countries, however, have yet to engage the Ukrainians directly on defense cooperation. In sum, the transatlantic partners have done far less to respond to Ukraine's defense requests than similar requests coming from Central and Eastern Europe. So far, that gap hasn't been that consequential thanks to the incredible restraint that the Ukrainian military has shown in dealing with tensions both inside and around its borders. We should caution, however, against relying on that continued restraint, especially in light of Russia's latest tactics in eastern Ukraine. It is not unimaginable that Ukraine could soon face a very serious military threat to the rest of its territory from the tens of thousands of Russian forces assembled on its border. For that reason, the United States should accelerate its reviews of Ukrainian military requests and determine what steps might be taken as soon as possible. Europeans—primarily the more capable ones—should be encouraged to assist with those efforts. Some capabilities obviously require substantial training but that does not apply in all cases, particularly in regard to requests for ammunition, intelligence sharing or training.

TRANSATLANTIC EFFORTS TO DATE MUST BE CONSIDERED THE OPENING ACT

Europe and the United States deserve some credit for their joint efforts in recent weeks to reassure allies in Central and Eastern Europe and support the interim government of Ukraine. NATO and the EU also merit kudos. But the real test will be whether the initiatives to date can be paired with a longer term strategy for enhancing engagement in the region and pairing that strategy with real capabilities and financial and political assistance. More importantly, the two partners must correct the mistake they made before the Russian annexation of Crimea and take the time now to outline the various scenarios they may be facing in the not too distant future. Are there high-level consultations among Europeans, Americans, and Ukrainians about how they would respond to Russian troops moving into eastern Ukraine? Are the partners thinking about the consequences of delayed Ukrainian elections? How would Europe and the United States react if Russia were to take steps to further destabilize Transnistria? A failure to plan now for such future scenarios risks leaving Europe and the United States unprepared and would send all the wrong signals to an already overconfident President Putin.

I look forward to answering any questions you might have.

_____

End Notes

[1] James Neuger, "NATO Reassures East Allies as it Questions Russian Pullback," Bloomberg, April 01, 2014.

[2] In 1990, in an effort to secure Soviet approval for German reunification, the parties participating in the Two Plus Four talks agreed that NATO troops and nuclear weapons would not be stationed in Eastern Europe. NATO repeated that promise in 1997 during the first round of NATO enlargement when it stated that it had "no intentions, no plans, and no reason" to send substantial numbers of troops and military assets to countries bordering the former Soviet Union.

[3] Bruno Waterfield and Tony Paterson, "Ukraine Crisis: Poland Asks NATO to Station 10,000 Troops on Its Territory," The Telegraph, April 01, 2014.

[4] Spiegel Staff, "Ukraine Crisis Exposes Searching for Deterrence: Gaps Between Berlin and NATO," Der Spiegel Online, April 07, 2014.

[5] Matthew Karnitschnig, "Germany's Angela Merkel Treads Softly With Russia's Putin On Ukraine," The Wall Street Journal, April 7, 2014.

[6] Carol Williams, "Ukraine Needs $35 Billion in Aid to Avert Default, Interim Leaders Say," Los Angeles Times, Feb 24, 2014.

[7] Daniela Schwarzer and Constanze Stelzenmuller, "What Is At Stake In Ukraine: Europe and the United States Need to Do What It Takes to Protect the Right of the Eastern Partnership Countries to Choose Their Future," German Marshall Fund of the United States, European Policy Paper 1/2014 (March 2014).

Senator MURPHY. Mr. Brzezinski.

STATEMENT OF IAN BRZEZINSKI, RESIDENT SENIOR FELLOW, BRENT SCOWCROFT CENTER ON INTERNATIONAL SECURITY, ATLANTIC COUNCIL, WASHINGTON, DC

Mr. BRZEZINSKI. Chairman Murphy, Ranking Member Johnson, I am honored to speak at this hearing on Central and Eastern Europe.

Russia's coercion and invasion of Ukraine presents a significant challenge to the security of Europe and to U.S. leadership and credibility. To date, the West has yet to generate a response that is likely to deter Moscow from further aggression.

The actions of the United States in this crisis should be guided by three mutually reinforcing objectives: to deter Russia from further aggression against Ukraine and other neighboring countries, to reinforce Ukraine's confidence in its capacity for self-defense, and to assist Ukraine in its effort to become a modern, prosperous democratic European state. Allow me to briefly review six realms of initiatives that serve these objectives.

First, we need firmer economic sanctions against Russia. The current set are clearly insufficient. Their overly selective scope has created little more than badges of courage among Russia's crony elite rather than the systemic economic pain necessary to make an authoritarian regime rethink its actions.

Second, the West's economic and diplomatic sanctions need to be complemented by a robust strategy to shore up NATO's allies in Ukraine. NATO's response to the invasion of Ukraine has been underwhelming. It has been limited to brooding ministerials, taskings of force posture studies, and a largely symbolic reinforcement of NATO air space. This underwhelming response reinforces concern about NATO's ability to act decisively, about the U.S. pivot to Asia, and about the reduction of U.S. combat capability in Europe. It affirms those who say Washington's commitment has declined.

The United States and NATO should reinforce Central European allies in the following ways. It should deploy now a ground combat brigade with air support to Poland and Romania. It should deploy special operation contingents to the Baltic States. The alliance should rescind the provision in the 1997 NATO-Russia Founding Act that asserts the alliance has no intention to base significant military combat presence in Central Europe. The United States should freeze the reduction of U.S. forces in Europe and direct EUCOM to present options to make permanent the deployments I just suggested. And our West European allies should be encouraged to do the same. These steps would help generate a context of security and confidence to Ukraine's immediate west.

Third, we need to provide military assurance to Ukraine. To date, NATO and the United States have unwisely drawn a redline on the alliance's eastern frontier, a redline that leaves Kiev militarily isolated.

That redline can and should be erased in the following ways. We should grant Ukraine's request for military equipment immediately and include antitank and antiaircraft weapons. U.S. equipment, I might add, would re-animate in Moscow unpleasant memories of when Soviet forces encountered them in Afghanistan.

We should deploy to Ukraine intelligence and surveillance capabilities and military trainers. This would force Moscow to consider the repercussions of any actions it takes affecting that presence. The United States deployment of military trainers to Georgia after it was invaded by Russia contributed usefully to that country's security. And, we should conduct now a major military exercise in Ukraine to help train its military. Waiting until June, as is currently planned by NATO, only incentivizes Russia to take military action earlier. None of these initiatives would threaten Russian territory. They would, however, introduce uncertainty in Moscow's military planning and force it to consider the risks of a costly and prolonged military conflict should it further its invasion of Ukraine.

Fourth, the West needs to reinforce Ukraine's resilience to Russia's propaganda campaign, which is the most intense we have seen since the end of the cold war. I am glad to hear Secretary Nuland outline actions that were taken, but I wonder if it is sufficient. This campaign threatens Ukraine's ability to conduct free and fair elections, it weakens the political unity required for Ukraine to undertake necessary and painful economic reforms, and it creates opportunity for the provocateurs Moscow has sent to the country.

Fifth, we need to support Ukraine's effort to reform its economy and integrate into Europe. Washington has done well in mobilizing international financial support for Ukraine. One area where we can do more is supporting the diversification of Ukraine's energy supplies and the integration of Ukraine's energy market into that of Europe. Freeing up U.S. LNG exports, to that they can be accessed by Central and Eastern Europe, would serve this priority.

And finally, the West needs to reanimate the vision of a Europe whole and free. The situation in Eastern Europe today necessitates that NATO make clear its open door policy is no passive phrase or empty slogan. Reaffirmation of this vision is an important way to underscore Washington's commitment to the security of Central and Eastern Europe.

And for these reasons, no decision or recommendation should be permitted or advanced that would in any way limit its applicability to any European country. Senator Johnson, that is why your concern about the proposal to "Finlandize" Ukraine is warranted. It would reward Putin for his aggression. It would bring us back to an age when great powers decided the futures of other countries. It would violate the spirit of the Maidon in which the Ukrainians went out and courageously articulated their desire to be part of Europe. Those wings should not be clipped at this point. And let me add we cannot really trust Putin to live up to such an agreement. A Ukraine that has had neutrality imposed upon would just encourage him to continue chipping away at its sovereignty and independence.

Let me conclude by saying the most effective way to counter Putin's hegemonic aspirations is to deny them opportunity for actualization. The presence of secure and prosperous democracies in Russia's neighborhood is not threatening, but it can help redirect Moscow's focus toward pressing internal problems. It may even provide momentum to those Russians who have grown wary of authoritarianism, corruption, and antiquated notions of empire.

Security in Central and Eastern Europe has always been essential to the forging of a true and enduring partnership between Europe and Russia and between Washington and Moscow.

Thank you.

[The prepared statement of Mr. Brzezinski follows:]

PREPARED STATEMENT IAN J. BRZEZINSKI

Chairman Murphy, Ranking Member Johnson, members of the committee, I am honored to speak at this hearing on the state of our interests in Central and Eastern Europe.

Russia's aggression against Ukraine presents a significant challenge to the security and stability of Europe and to U.S. leadership and credibility. For the second time in less than 6 years, Russia has invaded a neighboring country simply because that nation sought to move closer to Europe and to integrate itself into that community's multilateral organizations. As was the case with Russia's invasion of Georgia in 2008, the West has yet to generate a response to its seizure of Crimea that is likely to deter Moscow from further aggression against Ukraine or other states in Eastern Europe and along Russia's periphery.

The Kremlin's actions against Ukraine are but one element of a sustained revanchist policy that Vladimir Putin has articulated and exercised ever since he became President of Russia at the end of 1999. His objective has been to reestablish Russian hegemony, if not full control, over the space of the former Soviet Union. Toward this end, he has applied the full suite of Russian economic, energy, political, and military capacities to weaken and dominate neighboring states. He has leveraged information and cyber warfare, corruption and criminal networks, political provocateurs, separatist groups, frozen conflicts, and military incursions, among other means. His campaign history includes the 2007 cyber attack against Estonia, the separatist movement in Moldova, energy embargoes against Lithuania and Ukraine, and the aforementioned invasion of Georgia.

President Putin's strategy is one that pursues 20th-century objectives through 21st-century techniques and old-fashioned brute force. The implications of this most recent aggression against Ukraine include the following:

First, it is an unprovoked violation of the territorial sovereignty of a European nation—in this case the continent's second largest situated at the strategically significant crossroads of Europe and Eurasia.

Second, it undercuts efforts to curb the proliferation of weapons of mass destruction. Russia's seizure of Crimea is a direct violation of the 1994 Budapest Agreement in which Russia agreed to respect and protect Ukraine's territorial integrity in return for Kiev giving up the nuclear arsenal it inherited from the U.S.S.R.

Third, Putin's assertion that he has the unilateral right to redraw borders on the grounds that he is protecting ethnic Russians reintroduces into Europe a dangerous principle that provoked wars and caused countless deaths in earlier centuries and that we all hoped had been relegated to that past.

Fourth, Russia's incursion into Ukraine is a direct threat to the vision of Europe, whole, free, and secure. President Putin's objectives would create a new confrontational divide in Europe, between a community defined by self-determination, democracy, and rule of law and one burdened by authoritarianism, hegemony, and occupation.

Fifth, the aggression against Ukraine constitutes a challenge to the credibility of U.S. leadership. It serves Moscow's desire to portray Washington and NATO as lacking the diplomatic, economic, and military capability and will to counter effectively Russian power.

The response of the United States should be guided by three overlapping and mutually reinforcing objectives:

- To deter Russia from further aggression against Ukraine and other neighboring countries;
- To reinforce Ukraine's confidence in its capacity to defend itself; and,
- To assist Ukraine in its effort to become a modern, prosperous democratic European state.

These objectives can be pursued through immediate and longer term initiatives that will impose economic and geopolitical costs on Russia, increase the risks to Moscow of further provocative behavior, reinforce Central and Eastern Europe's sense of security, enhance Ukraine's capacity for defense, and help it transform into a successful, democratic, and prosperous European state. These include:

(1) *Firmer Economic Sanctions against Russia:* Current economic sanctions against Russia are clearly insufficient. Russian forces remain mobilized on Ukraine's border, the Kremlin still asserts the right to intervene in Ukraine, and its effort to destabilize Ukraine continues unabated.

Russia is a country that takes great pride in its history of enduring extreme economic hardship and military pain. It is not a polity where foreign economic sanctions against a limited set of Russian individuals and a bank or two will generate dynamics threatening to Putin's control in the near or medium term. The fact is that most of Russia today conducts business as usual, including with its American and European business partners. The overly narrow scope of these sanctions has let them be portrayed as badges of courage among Russia's crony elite rather than creating the systemic economic pain necessary to make an authoritarian regime rethink its actions.

Congress' provision to the president of authority to expand the set of sanctioned officials and entities to those involved in corruption should be leveraged immediately by the Obama administration. Widening the sanctions list is needed to have a more significant and immediate impact on Russia's financial operations, and the option Congress has offered cleverly ties those sanctions to a concern that generates real antigovernment outrage in the Russian population: corruption.

(2) *Strengthened Defense of Central Europe:* NATO's response to the invasion of Ukraine has been underwhelming. In its Crimea operation, Russia mobilized over 100,000 troops on its western frontier and invaded the peninsula with 20–30,000 troops. Today, tens of thousands of Russian soldiers backed by armor and air capacities are poised in high readiness on Ukraine's eastern borders.

Six weeks after the start of that invasion, the alliance's reaction is a largely symbolic reinforcement of Baltic, Polish, and Romanian airspace with NATO AWACS and a two-dozen allied aircraft, most of which are U.S. F–15s and F–16s. Washington also announced that it is sending 175 marines to its forward operating base in Romania and a ship to the Black Sea.

This hesitant response has been unnerving to NATO's Central European allies and partners. It has reinforced their concerns about NATO's ability to act decisively, about the United States declared "pivot to Asia," and over the reduction of U.S. combat capability in Europe. It strengthens the assertions of those who say that Washington's commitment to Europe's security has declined.

Immediate steps that should be taken by the United States and NATO to reinforce Central European allies include the following:

- The deployment of a brigade-level combat capability with air support to Poland and Romania. (This could involve the U.S. combat brigade team that the Department of Defense has regionally aligned for Europe.)

- The initiation of military exercises in the Baltic Sea and in the Baltic States and the deployment of special forces contingents to those countries.
- Rescinding the provision of the 1997 NATO-Russia Founding Act in which the alliance asserted that it had no need to permanently station significant combat capability on the territory of new NATO member states. As long as Crimea remains occupied by Russian forces, this policy, which was formulated in a time of partnership with Moscow, should be shelved.
- An immediate freeze of the execution of President Obama's 2012 decision to reduce U.S. combat capability in Europe and a reorientation of the U.S. European Command's on-going review that portends further reductions of U.S. forces and presence. That reorientation should be geared toward redefining EUCOM's requirements in the face of Russia's increasingly aggressive posture. Special consideration should be given to permanently deploying brigade-level combat capability in Central Europe, and our West European allies should be encouraged to do the same.

These immediate steps backed by the articulation of longer term force redeployment plans would build a context of security and confidence to Ukraine's immediate west. They are reasonable in light of Russia's long-term military buildup in the region and the magnitude of its aggression against Ukraine. They would constitute a clear setback for Moscow's regional aspirations, at least for those defined by President Putin.

(3) *Military Assurance to Ukraine:*[1] As NATO reinforces the territory of its member states, it also must bolster Ukraine's self-defense capability and self-confidence, and avoid steps that militarily isolate Kiev.

To date, NATO and the United States have done the latter. They have refused Ukraine's request for weapons that would help it better defend itself. NATO leaders, including President Obama, have publicly stated that they will not be drawn into a ''military excursion'' against Russia. This, in combination with the small scale of NATO's reinforcement of Central Europe, draws a redline, a limit to action, on the alliance's eastern frontier that in essence leaves Keiv to fend for itself.

It must be deeply disillusioning for Ukrainians who in recent months have so courageously expressed their desire for freedom and a place in Europe—and whose military are recently as November contributed to a NATO collective defense exercise, STEADFAST JAZZ. The West's self-imposed redline only reassures Vladimir Putin and his military planners, whose use in Crimea of unmarked military personnel—and the plausible deniability they provided—reflected at least initial concern about potential responses from NATO.

The following are defensive measures the United States and NATO can take to directly bolster Ukraine's security:

- Ukraine's request for military equipment should be immediately granted, and antitank and antiaircraft weapons should be included. Equipment and weapons could quickly be transferred from prepositioned U.S. military stocks in Europe. If NATO cannot attain the consensus to offer such help, then Washington should forge a coalition of the willing or act on its own. These weapons would complicate Russian military planning and add risk to its operations against Ukraine. U.S. equipment, in particular, would bring back unpleasant memories of when Soviet forces last encountered them in Afghanistan.
- The alliance or a U.S.-led coalition should deploy intelligence and surveillance capabilities and military trainers to Ukraine. This would provide needed situational awareness and help the Ukrainian military maximize its defensive capacities. It also would force Moscow to consider the potential political and military repercussions of any actions that affect that presence. The deployment of military trainers to Georgia was one of the more effective elements of the U.S. effort to bolster Georgia's security after it was invaded by Russia in 2008.
- NATO allies and partners should conduct now a military exercise in Ukraine as part of the effort to train the Ukrainian military. The alliance's plan to schedule exercises in Ukraine later in May and June seems to ignore Putin's timelines and could incentivize Russia to take additional military action before then.

Regarding this last recommendation, the NATO Response Force is well suited for such an operation. It was created to deploy on short notice a brigade-level force backed by combat air support. The NRF offers a means to demonstrate Western resolve prudently and rapidly. While it has the potential to significantly reinforce

---

[1] Parts of this section were adapted from Ian Brzezinski's ''Three Ways NATO can Bolster Ukraine's Security,'' The Washington Post, 25 March 2014.

Ukraine's defense against a sudden Russian offensive, it is certainly not big enough to jeopardize Russia's territorial integrity.

Each of these initiatives would complicate Putin's ambitions regarding Ukraine and could be executed in the near term. None would present a threat to Russia. They would, however, erase the redline the alliance has mistakenly created, assure Ukrainians that they are not alone, demonstrate that President Putin is unable to intimidate the West, and force Moscow to consider the possibility of a much more costly and prolonged military conflict.

(4) *Reinforced Public Diplomacy/Information Capability:* Another priority is countering Russia's significant propaganda effort to foster dissension and turmoil in Ukraine. As long as President Putin has been in power, Russia has used its formidable state-controlled media, which is widely distributed in Ukraine, to influence Ukrainian political events, including elections. Since the November outbreak of protests in Kiev against then-President Yanukovych, Moscow has turned up its disinformation war against Ukraine to a level not seen since the cold war.

Left unaddressed, this campaign threatens Ukraine's ability to conduct a free and fair election in May for a new President. It weakens the political unity Ukraine needs to undertake necessary and painful economic reforms, and it creates opportunity for the often-violent provocateurs Moscow has sent into the country.

Congress is to be commended for directing resources to reinforce U.S. public broadcasting in the region. It is an important step in strengthening Kiev's resilience against information warfare. Expanding Ukrainian, U.S., and international dissemination of accurate, credible information and news through all forms of media throughout Ukraine and increasing the presence of international observers there is essential to neutralizing Russia's efforts to destabilize Ukraine.

(5) *Support to Ukraine's Economic Transformation and Integration into Europe:* Ukraine's emergence as a stable and secure part of Europe is, of course, not just a military issue. It will require Ukraine to evolve into a prosperous and fully democratic polity, characterized by freedom and rule of law. In the context of Russia's military aggression, that transformation is particularly challenging and will require significant Western economic assistance.

The West, with U.S. leadership, has done well in mobilizing international financial support for Ukraine. The evolving IMF loan package, the European Union's assistance package and contributions by others in the international community, including by the United States and this Congress, promises Ukraine a needed foundation upon which to launch long-overdue fundamental reform.

One realm of economic transformation meriting further U.S. Government action is the diversification of Ukraine's energy supplies and its integration into the European energy market. Allowing the nations of Central and Eastern Europe direct and unfettered access to U.S. liquefied natural gas (LNG) exports would significantly enhance energy security in the region including that of Ukraine. It would undercut Moscow's excessive leverage in their gas markets.

Increased access to LNG would help drive forward infrastructure plans and investments that are linking the energy markets of this region and integrating them into that of Western Europe. It would enhance the prospects of the North-South gas corridor in Central Europe linking the Adriatic and Baltic Seas, offshoots of which would tie into Ukraine's pipeline network. Access to cheaper, reliably sourced energy would serve this region as a powerful economic stimulus.

Europe's need for U.S. energy exports has never been more urgent. A decision today to allow such exports would immediately send to allies and adversaries a powerful political signal of transatlantic solidarity. In the medium and long term, it would serve as a cornerstone of a transatlantic energy market that can only reinforce the solidarity of this important community of democracies.

(6) *Reanimating the Vision of Europe Whole and Free:* One of the key principals guiding U.S. policy toward Central and Eastern Europe since the fall of the Berlin Wall has been the vision of Europe, undivided, secure, and free. The West, led by the United States, must ensure that this vision is neither weakened nor perceived as having been derailed by Moscow's intimidation.

NATO will, in all likelihood, conduct its summit meeting in Cardiff, UK, this September in the context of Russia's provocative aggression against Ukraine. In addition to addressing its defense capabilities and the credibility of its Article V commitment to its member states, the alliance should use the moment to reanimate the process of NATO enlargement.

NATO must make clear that its ''open-door policy'' for membership is no passive phrase or empty slogan. Toward, that end, it should extend an invitation to Montenegro, a country that has made significant progress since 2009 under the alliance's Membership Action Plan.

Reaffirmation of Washington's adherence to this vision is an important way to underscore Washington's commitment to the security of Central and Eastern Europe. And, for these reasons, no decision or recommendation should be permitted or advanced that would in anyway limit its applicability to any country of Europe.

CONCLUSION

The absence of a firm Western response to Russia's invasion of Ukraine will only encourage Putin to act aggressively, be it to drive deeper into Ukraine, make another attempt to seize Georgia, expand Russia's occupation of Moldovan territory or grab other areas that were once part of the Soviet Union.

The steps outlined above are prudent, defensive, mutually reinforcing and consistent with the aspirations of the Ukrainian people to live in peace, in freedom, and as part of Europe.

By enhancing the security of Ukraine and the region, they will contribute substantively to a context favorable for genuine and enduring cooperation with Russia. The most effective way to counter President's Putin's hegemonic aspirations is to deny them opportunity for actualization. Russia will not be threatened by, but can only benefit from, having secure and prosperous democracies in its neighborhood. Such a development will help redirect the focus of authorities in Moscow to Russia's pressing internal problems. It may even provide momentum for those Russians who have grown weary of authoritarianism, corruption and antiquated notions of empire. Security in Central and Eastern Europe has always been the most effective way to forge a true and enduring partnership between Europe and Russia, and between Washington and Moscow.

Senator MURPHY. Thank you. I will turn the panel over to Mr. Chow, and I am going to turn the gavel over to Senator Cardin.

Mr. Chow.

STATEMENT OF EDWARD C. CHOW, SENIOR FELLOW, ENERGY AND NATIONAL SECURITY PROGRAM, CENTER FOR STRATEGIC AND INTERNATIONAL STUDIES, WASHINGTON, DC

Mr. CHOW. Thank you, Mr. Chairman, Ranking Member Johnson, Senator Cardin. I am honored to return to this committee 2 years after testifying before you on the serious and growing energy vulnerability of Ukraine, which is much in the news today.

My fellow panelists have covered very well the various hard and soft security challenges for Central and Eastern Europe. Since my own competence is limited to energy, I will focus on the threats and opportunities that sector presents to this region.

The legacy of the Warsaw Pact and Comecon left most of these countries reliant on Russia for their oil, gas, and nuclear fuel supplies, which were conducted under barter and other nonmarket trading terms. Transforming a highly inefficient and polluting energy economy necessitated a painful transition along with overall economic restructuring. Historical suspicion in the actual use of energy as a political tool by Russia gave further impetus to the drive to modernize the energy economy.

In general, countries that chose a speedier path for transition, full privatization of previously state-owned energy assets, introduction of market competition, and transparent regulation by independent bodies, adoption of European standards and business practices are in better condition today than those countries with state-owned companies that retained old business practices and relationships with their traditional supplier of imported fuels.

State companies in these countries continue to dominate the energy sector so that politics rather than market forces determine outcomes. Countries that have a coastline and, therefore, better access to crude oil and petroleum product imports from the international market and countries with significant indigenous energy production, such as Poland with coal and Romania with oil and gas, are less vulnerable to supply cutoffs.

Preemptive action also mitigated vulnerability to cutoffs. The Czech Republic's decision to build an oil pipeline from Bavaria in the mid-1990s is an example of a country which invested early on to reduce the risk of supply cutoffs. Until then, Czech refineries were totally dependent on crude supplies from the Soviet era Southern Druzhba pipeline from Russia and Ukraine. Poland and Lithuania's decision to commission liquefied natural gas receiving terminals are more recent examples of committed action to diversified energy supplies.

The potential for shale gas from a geological trend, which extends from southern Lithuania across Poland, Ukraine, Romania, to Bulgaria, offers good prospects for developing indigenous energy supply in the medium term that are affordable and environmentally beneficial.

European integration offers the best opportunity for energy modernization. The pathway to the European Union includes funds to assist reform and restructuring of the sector and to remove energy corruption by adopting European standards and business practices. The EU also offers funds for important infrastructure improvements, such as interconnector pipelines capable of reverse flows.

Market integration is critical for smaller countries in this region to achieve better diversity of energy supply. The energy industry relies on economy of scale to justify multibillion investments. Therefore, it is difficult for individual countries to economically justify diversification projects on their own without being connected to the energy markets of their neighbors with pipeline infrastructure, shared storage facilities, connected electricity grids, and sound commercial arrangements.

Unfortunately, the process of market integration has been painfully slow, and results have been mixed at best for the free flow of gas and electricity. Without market integration, the region simply cannot afford the energy supply diversity it wants.

Bulgaria is a prime example of a country which has not taken full advantage of a splendid geographic location and opportunities to connect with its neighbors in energy, failed to fully utilize EU accession funds for this purpose, stalled development of its shale gas potential, and is today not much better off than in 2006 and 2009, the last two gas cutoffs between Russia and Ukraine.

Since I testified previously before this subcommittee about the sorry state of the Ukrainian energy economy, and this topic came up in my testimony before the Senate Energy Committee 2 weeks ago, I will not spend much time talking about Ukraine here and leave this subject to the question period if Senators are interested.

Suffice it to say that Ukraine and its long, troubled gas relations with Russia remain the biggest supply vulnerability for the region. Half of Russian gas sales to all of Europe still transits Ukraine in spite of Russia's continuing efforts to bypass Ukraine. Ukraine is the dominant, in some cases the exclusive, route for gas imports to most Central and Southeastern European countries.

The potential benefits of energy sector reform in Ukraine remain enormous, and it is now more urgent than ever. There is much that countries from Central and Eastern Europe, which has gone through a successful transition to a modern energy economy, can offer Ukraine in terms of sharing lessons learned and assisting in capacity-building.

These are also countries which will be affected seriously by the possible collapse of the Ukrainian state. In many of these areas, it is natural for Europe to take the lead given its proximity and shared interest. However, the urgency and seriousness of the crisis in Ukraine demand American leadership and for us to coordinate our efforts with your European friends and with international financial institutions while enforcing strict compliance on the current and future governments of Ukraine to meet commitments to reform its critical energy sector as a condition for Western aid.

Thank you for your attention.

[The prepared statement of Mr. Chow follows:]

PREPARED STATEMENT OF EDWARD C. CHOW

Mr. Chairman, members of the committee, it is an honor for me to return to the European subcommittee 2 years after I testified before you on the serious, growing energy vulnerability of Ukraine, which is much in the news today.

My fellow panelists have already covered very well the various hard and soft security challenges for Central and Eastern Europe. Since my own competence is limited to energy, I will focus on the threats and opportunities that sector presents to countries in this region.

More than 20 years after the fall of the Iron Curtain and the transition from a command economy to a market economy, the energy economy of this region depends on three primary factors for each individual country:

    1. Geography and availability of indigenous energy sources;
    2. The state of modernization of the energy sector;
    3. European integration.

The legacy of the Warsaw Pact and Comecon left most of these countries reliant on Russia for its oil, gas, and nuclear fuel supplies, which were conducted under barter and other nonmarket trading terms, when they regained their full political independence. Transforming a highly inefficient and polluting energy economy necessitated a painful transition, along with overall economic restructuring. Historical suspicion and actual use of energy as a political tool by Russia gave further impetus to the drive for modernization of the energy economy.

In general, the countries that chose a speedier path for transition—full privatization of previously state-owned energy assets, introduction of market competition and transparent regulation by independent bodies, adoption of European standards and business practices—are in a better condition today than those countries with state-owned and controlled companies that maintain old business practices with traditional suppliers of imported fuels and continue to dominate the energy sector so that politics rather than market forces determine outcomes.

In general, countries with a coastline and better access to crude oil and petroleum imports and countries with significant indigenous energy production, such as Poland with coal and Romania with oil and gas, are less vulnerable to supply cutoffs. However preemptive action has also mitigated vulnerability to cutoffs. For example, the Czech Republic's courageous decision to build an oil pipeline from Bavaria (Ingolstadt-Kralupy-Litvinov) in the mid-1990s in midst of its breakup with Slovakia is an example of an inland country, which invested early on to reduce its vulnerability to supply cutoffs. Until then, Czech refineries were totally dependent on crude oil supplies from the Soviet-era Southern Druzhba pipeline from Russia and Ukraine. Poland and Lithuania's decisions to commission liquefied natural gas (LNG) receiving terminals are more recent examples of real action on commitment to diversify energy supplies.

The potential for shale gas from a geological trend, which extends from southern Lithuania, across Poland, Ukraine, Romania to Bulgaria, offers an excellent opportunity to develop indigenous energy resources in the medium term that are affordable and environmentally beneficial.

European integration offers the best opportunity for energy modernization. The pathway to the European Union includes funds to assist much-needed reform and restructuring of the sector, and removing corruption by adopting European standards and business practices. The EU also offers funds for important infrastructural improvements, such as interconnector pipelines capable of reverse flows.

Market integration is critical to the smaller countries in this region achieving better diversity of energy supply. The energy industry relies on economy of scale to justify multibillion dollar investments. The entire population of the Balkans is smaller than the population of Turkey. Therefore, it is difficult for individual countries in southeastern Europe to economically justify projects for supply diversity on their own without being connected to the energy markets of their neighbors with pipeline infrastructure, shared storage facilities, connected electric grids, and sound commercial arrangements.

Unfortunately, the process of market integration in this region has been painfully slow and results have been mixed at best. Without market integration, the region simply cannot afford the energy supply diversity it says it wants. Bulgaria is a prime example of a country which has not taken full advantage of its excellent geography and opportunities to connect with its neighbors in energy, failed to fully utilize EU accession funds for this purpose, has not developed its shale gas potential, and is today not much better off in terms of supply vulnerability from, let's say, a gas cutoff between Russia and Ukraine, than it was in 2006 and 2009.

Since I testified previously before this subcommittee about the sorry state of the Ukrainian energy economy and this topic came up in my testimony before the Senate Energy and Natural Resource Committee 2 weeks ago, I will not spend much time talking about Ukraine here and leave this subject to the question period if Senators are interested.

Suffice it to say that Ukraine and its troubling gas relations with Russia remains the most important example of supply vulnerability for countries in central and southeastern Europe. Half of Russian gas sales to Europe still transits Ukraine, in spite of Russia's continuing efforts to bypass Ukraine. Ukraine is the dominant, in some cases the exclusive, route for Russian gas supply to central and southeastern European countries which is also their sole import source.

The potential benefits of energy sector reform in Ukraine remains enormous and it is now more urgent than ever. There is much that countries from Central and eastern Europe, which has gone through a successful transition to a modern energy economy, can offer Ukraine in terms of sharing lessons learned and assisting in capacity-building. They are also the countries which will be most affected by the collapse of the Ukrainian state.

In many of these areas, it is natural for Europe to take the lead given its proximity and shared interests. However, given the urgency and seriousness of the crisis in Ukraine, the United States must play an important role and coordinate our efforts with our European friends and international financial institutions, while enforcing strict compliance on the current and future governments of Ukraine in meeting commitments to reform its critical energy sector as a condition for providing Western aid.

Senator CARDIN [presiding]. Thank you for your testimony. Thank all three of you for your testimony. Senator Johnson to inquire?

Senator JOHNSON. Thank you, Senator Cardin. Mr. Brzezinski, you obviously are recommending a more robust response than what we are seeing today. You also mentioned a more robust response than we are hearing that was actually implemented in Georgia. Can you just go in greater detail in terms of what the United States actually did versus what is being reported in the press nowadays and how that had an effect?

Mr. BRZEZINSKI. When I look back to the Georgia crisis, I cannot look back and say that was a successful example of the West's response to aggression by a great power against a small country that supported us in Afghanistan and elsewhere. But some of the things that we did do right include the following.

One, we demonstrated we are willing to take military risk. So, for example, when the Chairman of the Joint Chiefs of Staff, Admiral Mullen, called his Russian counterpart and said that we are going to fly back, in United States military aircraft, the Georgian troops serving in Iraq or Afghanistan, the Russian general threatened to shoot down the U.S. transport aircraft—this is documented in a New York Times article. Admiral Mullen responded swiftly and firmly, stating simply that this would be a mistake. The planes will be flying to Georgia. That was a signal to the Russians that the United States was serious.

The second thing we did to assure the Georgians was to provide them military equipment, including arms. We deployed trainers in Georgia. These marines who went out there and deployed were embedded in the Georgian military units they were training, which raised the prospect of them getting caught up in any sort of action the Russians might take against the Georgians. That was an important deterrent.

Senator JOHNSON. Do you recall the numbers?

Mr. BRZEZINSKI. No, I do not.

Senator JOHNSON. Okay.

Mr. BRZEZINSKI. They were not high, so it does not take a huge amount. But it takes demonstration of resolve and commitment, and today we have not done that. As you pointed out, in the beginning of the Ukraine crisis, the Russians mobilized 100,000 troops in the Western frontier. They deployed 20,000 to 30,000 special forces into Crimea. And what has the West done? Our response is five or six F–15s to the Baltics, a dozen or so F–16s to Western Poland, and defensive AWAC flights along the Romanian and Polish frontiers, and I understand also a company of marines to Romania. That is about it. That is not significant. That is not a demonstration of resolve. That communicates hesitancy to the Russians.

Senator JOHNSON. In your written testimony, you were talking—described in greater detail the types of military support you would provide to the Ukrainian military. Can you just speak to that now?

Mr. BRZEZINSKI. The Ukrainian military is about 129,000 with roughly 80,000 being ground forces. They are not the most highly equipped. They are not the most highly ready, but they should not be underestimated. They have had 20 years of independence. They have been in NATO operations. They have a joint battalion or brigade with the Poles. They trained in NATO standards.

They are more ready than most people expect. They are capable of taking on Western equipment. I think they should be given equipment that would help mitigate Russia's strengths in armor and aircraft. So antitank weapons would be useful, antiaircraft weapons would be useful. Now, that would not guarantee them the ability to survive a massive onslaught by the Russians, but it sure as heck would make it really, really painful for the Russians, and that should make the Russians think twice. Right now Moscow does not have to think that way.

Senator JOHNSON. It might change the calculus. Ms. Smith, would you disagree with what Mr. Brzezinski is talking about?

Ms. SMITH. Well, as I stated earlier, I do think the administration needs to ramp up its review of the defense requests that have come in to date. I would note that to date, it is a mix of lethal and nonlethal requests. I have not seen specific requests for antitank weapons. I have seen ammunition, small arms as you had mentioned, Senator, as well as some of the nonlethal support. I do think specifically what would be extremely helpful would be on the intel-sharing side, and as Ian pointed out, training will be absolutely indispensable moving forward.

Senator JOHNSON. I mean, part of the problem is when we heard this actually from the Prime Minister himself, they are very reluctant to ask for something they know would not be supplied. I mean, they are intelligent enough about that, so that is part of the problem.

Mr. Chow, I read a very interesting op-ed in the Wall Street Journal talking about LNG permits and the applications for them here. And the point being made there is just simply allowing the application process to go through on those LNG terminals would send a pretty strong signal and have an effect, even though the LNG would not flowing for a while. Would you agree or disagree with that assertion?

Mr. CHOW. Thank you, Senator, for the question. I think from an LNG export policy standpoint and for an oil export policy standpoint for that matter, there are plenty of reasons why the United States should reexamine our existing policy and laws on energy exports given that they were mainly written in the 1970s at a time where energy scarcity was the driving motivation for the legislation. And those issues are being discussed properly in Congress and reviewed and this reexamination should take its course. So I am in favor of the idea of looking at the level of LNG and other energy exports again.

My concern is trumpeting a tool that is ineffective, in the short to medium term, may have counterproductive consequences. Ukraine does not have an LNG terminal. If it were to have one and the Turks were to allow LNG tankers to go through the Bosporus, it would take at least 2 years to build. We do not have any capability of sending any LNG until maybe 2016, and the volume of capacity that the Department of Energy has already approved is quite robust already. It is about 95 billion cubic meters per year, more than the consumption of Germany.

So what we are doing is already having an effect, but to threaten the Russians with something that they know cannot happen for 2 or 3 years may be counterproductive. And my reaction as an energy person is to say that the Russian reaction would be ''if that is the best you have got, then we have nothing to worry about.''

Senator JOHNSON. Okay. Well, thank you all for your testimony.

Senator CARDIN. Once again, thank you. Mr. Chow, let me just follow up on that for a moment if I might, and that is you mentioned that any solution with LNG in regards to Ukraine would be mid-term and long-term solutions, not just short-term. Can you just review with us what we should be doing in the short term?

Russia has a double-edged sword here. They can absolutely apply different pressure on Ukraine by either raising prices or cutting off, but it is a very profitable source of income for Russia. And, of course, a lot of the energy goes through the pipelines to other countries. However, Ukraine needs to make itself more independent and have alternative sources of energy and ultimately use less energy, which is an area that, I think, the IMF is very interested in— energy conservation and the fact that there is a lot of wasted energy. And of course the pricing to the consumer has not been reflective of the cost.

The IMF is instituting certain reforms where there will be better pricing, and some of the IMF support will go to low income families to make it more affordable. But do you have other suggestions as to how Ukraine could become less vulnerable to Russian pressure in the short term on energy?

Mr. CHOW. Yes, sir. Ukraine is not without leverage on its energy gas relationship with Russia. Even today more than 50 percent of Russia's exports to Europe, which, as you pointed out, is this prime market for gas exports, go through Ukraine.

The problem in the past 20-some years is that that leverage has been used by individual Ukrainian politicians for private profit or corruption rather than for state interests. So even today the Ukraine has the means—has the leverage to stabilize its gas transit and supply relationship with Russia if the overall political relations were to calm down.

But in order to do that, it needs to remove the pervasive corruption in the energy sector in the Ukraine, particularly on gas. And one thing I would do for sure is to completely restructure the national oil and gas company, Naftohaz, which is at the center of that corrupt practice.

The other thing I would do in addition to what the IMF rightfully has done in terms of getting market clearing prices on the consuming side for gas is also to increase wellhead gas prices. What is happening today is that, if you are a domestic producer of gas in Ukraine, you are getting a small fraction of the price that Ukraine pays Russia even 3 months ago. That is a disincentive to produce more domestic energy.

And one might question why it is the way it is. Well, you know, multitier pricing helps create a gray market for gas domestically in Ukraine, with once again privileged access for politically connected folks who are the ones who benefit from it. The rest of the Ukrainian public suffers shortages, even though they are the ones who are supposedly benefiting from the low prices. So pricing reform is key to reform, but not just at the burner tip, but also at the wellhead.

Senator CARDIN. Thank you for that. I think they are all important points about the economics of the issues. But still I would hope that we would look at alternative sources other than Russian energy in the event that there are short-term strategies deployed by Russia to impose a crisis in Ukraine. I understand it would also hurt Russia, and I fully appreciate the reforms that are needed in the energy sector. I could not agree with you more, but I think your points are very well taken.

Let me shift gears to the security issues. And I followed with great interest the testimony on the seriousness that Russia takes the commitment to defend territories, whether it be Ukraine or the countries in that region. And, yes, one thing we know, Russia does not want to see NATO expanded on their borders. They do not want to see troops on their borders. They are very concerned about that. That was the agreement that was reached that we would not station there.

I think, though, they are very much aware of our treaty commitments to NATO allies, so I really do think that is a consideration even for a person like Mr. Putin before he would take action against a NATO ally. But there are other countries in that region that are not NATO allies. Georgia is interested in becoming a NATO partner. That would present a very interesting dynamic to Russia. Ukraine is a little bit early. They have not moved in that direction. Russia certainly does not want to see Ukraine become a NATO partner.

But I think moving in that direction would be exactly what Russia does not want to see happen. And it would be interesting from the point of view of trying to counter what Russia is doing today if there were more interest in more common defense, such as NATO, in regards to that region.

So I would just like to get your views as to NATO expansion. Europe has been reluctant on NATO expansion for reasons unrelated to the Russian created crisis. There will be a meeting later this year in which there will be considerations of countries for NATO accession.

What is your view as to how helpful that would be in making it clear to Russia that we are very serious about protecting the territorial integrity of countries in the region?

Ms. SMITH. Well, thank you, Senator, for that question. You are right, the one fundamental question is what does Russia want, and you are absolutely 100 percent right in your assessment. The Russians clearly do not want to see any additional rounds of NATO enlargement.

The other question, of course, is what does NATO want. And the answer to that on NATO enlargement depends on who you ask, as you rightly pointed out. This is a controversial subject. There is a divide. Part of the alliance is not prepared to advance forward with NATO enlargement. I think the United States feels quite passionate about the fact that the door remains open and that we should not give a country like Russia any sort of veto over this process whatsoever.

There is also the question of what a country like Georgia wants and what it deserves. In my personal view, I think we have come so far down this road with a country like Georgia, it is hard to figure out how we would ever exit. I would not recommend we would exit, but I think there are countries inside the alliance that would be comfortable prolonging this process forever.

But if you look at the sacrifices that Georgian soldiers have made in a place like Afghanistan, and all they have done as a true blue partner to the NATO alliance, and how they have worked to meet the criteria for membership, to me it is unimaginable that we could slow down this process. Personally I advocate for Georgia to move forward with MAP at the next summit. But again, I am skeptical whether or not we will succeed in doing that because there appears to be a great deal of hesitation, particularly across some countries in Western Europe to do that.

I recognize that that would add an additional security burden to the alliance, but what better sign of our commitment from Europe and the United States to a country like Georgia then to move forward with MAP?

Senator CARDIN. Just add to your answer before turning to Mr. Brzezinski. What do you think Russia's reaction to NATO expansion in Georgia would mean?

Ms. SMITH. It could be quite devastating. I mean, emotionally and symbolically they will raise a complete stink about this, and they will cry foul on all accounts. It is not the same as us stationing ground troops in a place like Poland where they will say, hey, in 1997 you promised not to do that. There is nothing we ever said about stopping NATO enlargement. We never made that promise, so they cannot claim that.

They will claim that we are infringing on their security, that we are trying to encircle them, trying to contain them. There will be all sorts of complaints. But the question here is whether or not we would see Russian irritation, tension in the relationship, additional further Russian aggression if we did not do it. And that is the question inside the alliance. Half of the alliance thinks that this will provoke additional Russian aggression. Some say, no, it will prevent it if we move forward with MAP for Georgia, and I fall in that category.

Senator CARDIN. Thank you. Mr. Brzezinski.

Mr. BRZEZINSKI. Let me just add a couple of points because I think what Julie says is accurate. There is great division in the alliance. In fact, there is probably be a predisposition in the alliance against further enlargement for the reasons she puts. Part of it is because this administration has not pushed for NATO enlargement. So in the absence of strong U.S. leadership and support of enlargement, it is not surprising it withers on the side of Europe.

The second point I would make is that NATO is on Russia's border. As you know, Norway is on Russia's border. Estonia is on Russia's border. And membership in NATO has not undercut relations between those two countries and Russia. In fact, Norway, which has a very good relationship with Russia and is very proud of their cooperation in the Arctic, for example, and it is a stalwart NATO member. Poland, a country that has had a troubled history with Russia, actually had an improvement—a significant improvement in its relationship with Russia ever since it became a member of NATO.

So there is not a real track record of NATO membership undercutting a relationship with Russia. What has undercut Russia's relationship with the West and NATO is President Putin and his aspirations for an antiquated notion of empire, a dominion over the space of the former Soviet Union, if not control over that space. And that is the problem that we have.

I think if we are going to counter that, the most effective way is to continue the process of enlarging Europe, of extending EU membership to countries, of steadily pushing NATO for the countries that seek it and that are ready for it. It provides security. It is nonthreatening to others. It is a solid foundation stone for actually a context of enduring cooperation with Russia.

As Julie points out, we want to eliminate gray zones from Europe. Gray zones are like walls: they create separation and distance. If we can bring communities of democracies closer together and enhance their security, we are all better off, including Russia.

Senator CARDIN. Thank you. I think that is very helpful. And again, I thank all three of you for your testimony. This is an issue that is going to be around for a while. Unfortunately we have frozen conflicts in Georgia, Moldova, and Azerbaijan. And it looks like it is getting pretty cold in Crimea. So it looks like we are going to be with this for a while. There is certainly a lot of provocative action by Russia in Eastern Ukraine, and there is concern in other areas that Russia is very much planning for additional military options.

So this issue is very fluid. And I can tell you I think there is very strong support in Congress to make it clear that we will not ever accept the grab by Russia—what it is doing in the Ukraine or any other country.

So I thank you all for helping the record of this committee. And with that, the subcommittee will stand adjourned. Thanks.

[Whereupon, at 4:43 p.m., the hearing was adjourned.]